Author

Yevheniy Haydanka

SPECTRUM SLOVAKIA Series
Volume 50

Political Fragmentation
of the Slovak Republic
in Light of Regional Elections

PETER LANG   VEDA

Bibliographic Information published by the Deutsche Nationalbibliothek
The Deutsche Nationalbibliothek lists the publication in the Deutsche Nationalbibliografie; detailed bibliographic data is available in the internet at http://dnb.d-nb.de.

Author: Yevheniy HAYDANKA
            Associate Professor at the Department of Political Science, PhD.
            University of Trnava, Trnava, Slovakia

Reviewers: Anatoliy ROMANYUK, Dr. Sc., Professor,
           Lviv National Ivan Franko University, Lviv, Ukraine

           Yuriy OSTAPETS, Dr. Sc., Professor,
           Uzhhorod National University, Uzhhorod, Ukraine

ISSN 2195-1845
ISBN 978-3-631-93944-4   ISBN 978-80-224-2114-0
ePDF 978-3-631-93962-8
ePub 978-3-631-93963-5
DOI 10.3726/b23007

© 2025 Peter Lang Group AG,   © VEDA, Publishing House
Lausanne   of the Slovak Academy of Sciences
Published by Peter Lang GmbH,   Bratislava 2025
Berlin, Germany

www.peterlang.com   www.veda.sav.sk

Contents

Contents

Introduction

The enhancement of regional institutions was a primary focus for the Slovak authorities prior to its accession to the EU. This included the transfer of authority from the central government to regional bodies, facilitating the political empowerment of newly established regional authorities such as Regional Assemblies and Župans. The initiation of electoral processes at the regional level in 2001 led to a significant fragmentation of the regions within the Slovak Republic. Varying support for different political parties/ electoral coalitions or candidates for the post of Župan is indicative of the diverse ideologies held by Slovak voters. The capital region, western regions, north, centre, and east of the country frequently demonstrated differing preferences in the election of regional authorities. This diversity was evident in the support for more conservative or liberal politicians, pro-European forces or Eurosceptic parties, as well as pro-government or opposition candidates for the post of Župan.

The present book identifies several objectives aimed at facilitating an assessment of the level of political fragmentation among the regions of the Slovak Republic based on recent regional elections. This entails defining the legal framework of the administrative-territorial system of the Slovak Republic, conducting an analysis of the electoral processes, evaluating the course and outcomes of regional elections from 2001 to 2017, and determining the political fragmentation of the regions of the Slovak Republic using the results of the 2022 regional elections. The first chapter, will explore the administrative, territorial, and electoral foundations of Slovak regionalism. The analysis will encompass the legislative framework for the administrative-territorial division in the Slovak Republic, the delineation of the territorial hierarchy within the country, and the variances in regional GDP. Of particular focus will be the elucidation of electoral legislation governing the election of Regional Assemblies and Župans. Additionally, by comparing voter turnout across the spectrum of all election types in the Slovak Republic, the chapter will illustrate the level of electoral engagement in regional elections.

An analysis of the political landscape in the regions of the Slovak Republic was conducted, focusing on the 2022 elections. The initial regional elections, which were held in 2001 following decentralization, played a pivotal role in consolidating electoral process-

es at the regional level. These elections underscored the rivalry between pro-Mečiar and anti-Mečiar political forces. Subsequently,
the 2005 regional elections assumed institutional importance in
the context of Slovakia's regional politics following its accession
to the EU. During this period, the influence of the SMER-SD Party
on the Regional Assembly began to increase. Finally, in 2009, the
conservative-populist union ĽS-HZDS–SMER-SD emerged triumphant in the elections. The capital Bratislava region is notably dis-
tanced from the rest of the Slovak regions in terms of electoral
preference. In the 2013 regional elections, SMER-SD solidified its
political dominance across the majority of regions. The 2017 regional elections were marked by significant surprises, including
independent MPs prevailing over traditional political parties and
coalitions. Furthermore, the longstanding tenure of "life-long"
Župans came to an end, with new Župans elected through single-
round elections.

The final chapter carefully examines the attributes of the 2022
regional elections. The authorities in Slovakia made the decision
to unite the regional and local elections, resulting in significant
changes in the political landscape of the regions. The protracted
political crisis in the Slovak Republic had a direct impact on the
outcome of the regional elections. Once more, the voting displayed
the decreasing confidence of Slovak voters in political parties.
Conversely, the support for independent candidates began to
grow. To elucidate the ongoing political fragmentation in Slovak
regions, two political cleavages were identified: "Slovak Politics vs
Hungarian Minority" and "Party vs Independent Deputies".

Abbreviations

ANO (slov. – *Aliancia nového občana*) – Alliance of the New Citizen

DS (*Demokratická strana*) – Democratic Party

DÚ (*Demokratická únia*) – Democratic Union

EPP – European People's Party

EU – European Union

FIDESZ (hu. – *Fidesz – Magyar Polgári Szövetség*) – Hungarian Civic Alliance

HZD (*Hnutie za demokraciu*) – Movement for Democracy

HZDS (*Hnutie za demokratické Slovensko*) – Movement for a Democratic Slovakia

KDH (*Kresťanskodemokratické hnutie*) – Christian Democratic Movement

KDS (*Konzervatívni demokrati Slovenska*) – Conservative Democrats of Slovakia

LAU – Local Administrative Units

ĽB (*Ľavicový blok*) – Left Bloc

LIGA – Liga Party

ĽS-HZDS (*Ľudová strana – Hnutie za demokratické Slovensko*) – People's Party — Movement for a Democratic Slovakia

ĽSNS (*Ľudová strana naše Slovensko*) – People's Party Our Slovakia

MKÖ-MKS (*Magyar Közösségi Összefogás – Maďarská komunitná spolupatričnosť*) – Hungarian Community Unity

MOST-HÍD – Bridge Party

NÁŠ KRAJ – Our Region Party

NEKA – Independents

NOVA (*Nová väčšina*) – New Majority

NUTS (fr. – *Nomenclature des Unités territoriales statistiques*) – Nomenclature of Territorial Units for Statistics

OKS (*Občianska konzervatívna strana*) – Civic Conservative Party

OĽaNO (*Obyčajní ľudia a nezávislé osobnosti*) – Ordinary People and Independent Personalities

PS (*Progresívne Slovensko*) – Progressive Slovakia

REPUBLIKA – Republic Movement

ŠANCA – CHANCE Party

SaS (*Sloboda a Solidarita*) – Freedom and Solidarity

SDK (*Slovenská demokratická koalícia*) – Slovak Democratic Coalition

SDKÚ-DS (*Slovenská demokratická a kresťanská únia – Demokra-*

tická strana) – Slovak Democratic and Christian Union – Democratic Party

SDĽ (*Strana demokratickej ľavice*) – Party of the Democratic Left

SF (*Slobodné fórum*) – Free forum

SIEŤ – NETWORK Party

SME RODINA – We Are Family

SMER-SD (*Smer – sociálna demokracia*) – Direction – Social Democracy

SMK-MKP (*Strana maďarskej komunity – Magyar Közösség Pártja*) – Party of the Hungarian Community

SMS (*Strana moderného Slovenska*) – Modern Slovakia Party

SNS (*Slovenská národná strana*) – Slovak National Party

SOM Slovensko – IAM Slovakia Party

SOP (*Strana občianskeho porozumenia*) – Party of Civic Understanding

SRK (*Strana rómskej koalície*) – Roma Coalition Party

SZ (*Strana zelených*) – Green Party

SZÖVETSÉG-ALIANCIA – Hungarian Alliance

SZS (*Strana zelených Slovenska*) – Slovak Green Party

ÚSVIT – Dawn Party

ZA ĽUDÍ – For the People

Zmena zdola – Change from Below Party

ZSNS (*Zjednotená Slovenská národná strana*) – United Slovak National Party

1 Regions, Regional Government, and Regional Elections in the Slovak Republic

1.1 Administrative and Territorial Foundations of Slovak Regionalism

During the early political transformations of the 1990s in the Czechoslovak Federation, a series of events led to the initiation of the first attempts at legislative regulation of Slovakia's territorial structure. The legislative initiative resulted in the creation of the first act regulating the issue of administrative-territorial division, referred to as "The Law on the Creation of Municipalities" (slov. – *"Zákon o obecnom zriadení"*), which was adopted in 1990 (Zákon č. 369/1990). The municipality is a self-governing entity that brings together at least 3,000 residents (§2a, 5). The Municipal Council, whose deputies are elected in direct elections for a period of four years, serves as the governing body of the municipality (§11, 1). The *Starosta*, a civil servant by profession, is responsible for the administration of the municipality (§13, 1) (Zákon č. 369/1990).

The issue of regionalization was first addressed in the electoral legislation of the Slovak Republic through the Law "On Elections to the National Council of Slovakia" (*"Zákon o voľbách do Slovenskej národnej rady"*), which was also adopted in 1990 (Zákon č. 80/1990). To ensure the smooth and effective conduct of parliamentary elections, four multi-mandate voting districts were established, namely: Bratislava, with its main centre located in the capital city of Bratislava; West Slovakia (*Západoslovenský kraj*); Central Slovakia (*Stredoslovenský kraj*); and East Slovakia (*Východoslovenský kraj*) (§9). Each of these electoral regions comprised several electoral districts (*volebné okrsky*) (Zákon č. 80/1990). The National Council held elections in such multi-mandate voting districts in 1990, 1992, and 1994. During the 1994 elections, the Bratislava multi-mandate voting districts comprised 363 voting districts, whereas the West Slovakia region had 1,758 constituencies, the Central Slovakia region had 1,894 constituencies, and the Eastern Slovak Region had 1,822 districts (Voľby a referendá). The modern Slovak Republic follows the administrative-territorial division typically found in EU member states (Refer to Table 1).

Table 1. Administrative Territorial Units of the Slovak Republic (as of 31 December, 2023).

NUTS-2 (Oblasť)	NUTS-3 (Kraj)	LAU-1 (Okres)	LAU-2 (Obec)
Bratislava	Bratislava region	8	89
Western Slovakia	Trnava region Nitra region Trenčín region	7 7 9	251 354 276
Central Slovakia	Žilina region Banská Bystrica region	11 13	315 516
Eastern Slovakia	Prešov region Košice region	13 11	665 461
Total	**8**	**79**	**2,927**

Source: the author's calculations are based on the data from the website of statistics of administrative and territorial units of the Slovak Republic OBCE SR (OBCE SR, 2024; NUTS Maps, 2023).

According to the Constitution of the Slovak Republic, municipalities (*obce*) are designated as the primary unit of local self-governance, while regions (*kraj*) are the territorial unit of regional self-governance (Art. 64) (Ústavný zákon č. 460/1992). The Law "On the Territorial and Administrative Organization of the Slovak Republic" of 1996 (*"Zákon o územnom a správnom uspo-riadaní Slovenskej republiky"*) clearly established the boundaries of eight regions, each of which was comprised of administrative units known as districts (*okresy*), as stipulated in §2, part 2 of the aforementioned law (Zákon č. 221/1996). Following the implementation of the decentralization reform, the regions were given distinct administrative and legal powers as higher self-government entities, whereas the districts were no longer tasked with acting as local executive and administrative authorities. The Law "On Self-Government of Higher Administrative Units" of 2001 (*"Zákon o sa-mospráve vyšších územných celkov (Zákon o samosprávnych kra-joch)"*) provides clear guidelines on the administrative-territorial boundaries of regions, the legal competence of governing bodies in regions, opportunities for international cooperation, and other related matters (Zákon č. 302/2001). The legal capacities of governing bodies in municipalities and regions are strengthened through the implementation of pertinent electoral processes. These processes include the election of self-governing bodies for municipalities and regions, which contribute to the enhancement of legal competence and overall governance.

In most cases, the legal capacity of the management bodies of the Regional Assembly and the degree of institutional autonomy in the regions are determined by the level of fiscal autonomy. The relevant Law of 2001 clearly defines the primary possibilities and limitations of fiscal autonomy in the regions (Zákon č. 302/2001). A self-governing region is a legally recognized entity that possesses the authority to autonomously manage its property and earnings (§1, 5). The administrative body of the self-governing region typically devises strategic plans for the region's social and economic advancement, executes its own investment and business policies, and oversees the functioning of its budgetary and profit-making organizations (§4, 1). In order to facilitate efficient regional economic policy, the self-governing region develops an annual budget. The primary sources of revenue for the regional budget include its own profits, subsidies from the state budget, and various other financing sources (§9). In relation to budget adoption, the Regional Assembly is endowed with primary powers. These include the adoption of the budget and its necessary modifications, as well as the control over the use of budget funds. Moreover, the Župan may also have the authority to make certain modifications to the budget (§9, d). The Chief Controller plays a vital role in the financial structure of the self-governing region by performing audit and control functions. The Regional Assembly elects the Chief Controller for a term of six years, as prescribed in §19a, 5. The Chief Controller is responsible for monitoring the execution of the budget, ensuring efficient management in the region, and conducting general control of revenues and expenditures in the regional budget, as outlined in §19c, 1 (Zákon č. 302/2001).

Based on the GDP per capita indicator, there is a noticeable disparity between the central region (capital area) and the outlying regions, which is illustrated in Figure 1.

The average GDP per capita in Slovakia as of 2022 was €19.975 (IBM Cognos Connection). Based on this key economic indicator, the regions of Slovakia have been stratified into three distinct groups, delineated by differences in their GDP per capita:

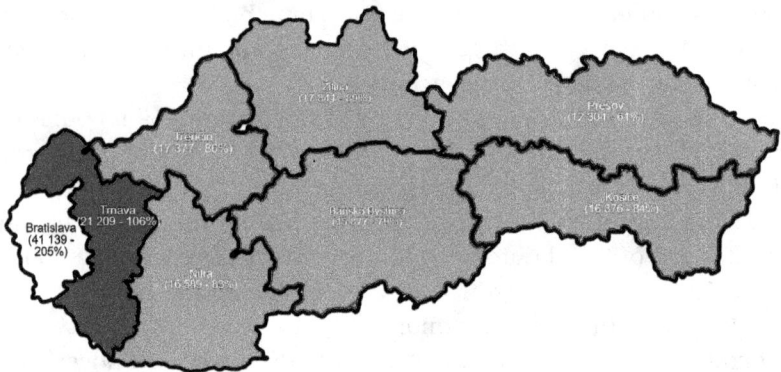

Figure 1. Distribution of GDP Per Capita by Region in Euros for 2022 in Slovakia[1].

Source: the author's calculations are based on the Statistical Office of the Slovak Republic (IBM Cognos Connection).

(1) Low GDP per capita (total negative indicator) – the Slovak Republic presents a situation where most of its regions are currently experiencing low GDP per capita, which is generally considered a negative economic indicator. Out of the eight regions, six have a GDP per capita that is below the national average. However, the two extreme western regions in the country are the only exceptions. It is noteworthy that this situation is true for the entirety of the Slovak Republic, with some discernible differentiation within the middle of this group. It is noteworthy, too, that the Prešov region is the weakest in terms of GDP, only meeting 61% of the national average. The Žilina region also lags behind, with a GDP per capita of only 89% of the national average. In general, the eastern part of the country and the mountainous Banská Bystrica region have the lowest economic performance in the country.

(2) Progressive GDP per capita (overall positive indicator) – the Trnava region is the only region belonging to this group. The term "Progressive GDP" refers to an economic indicator greater than 100% of the national indicator. This is an important benchmark for

---

1 When preparing the map, I used an image from the portal depicting the regions of the Slovak Republic, e.g. *Slovenská správa ciest*. Available at: https://www.cdb. sk/sk/Vystupy-CDB/Mapy-cestnej-siete-SR/Mapy-krajov.alej. The map illustrates the GDP per capita data in Euros for each region, along with the corresponding percentage of compliance with the average Slovak GDP per capita indicator.

objective comparisons with other regions that have a negative indicator, i.e. less than 100% of the national indicator. The Trnava region, located adjacent to the capital, Bratislava, and bordering Austria, the Czech Republic, and Hungary, has a cross-border location and is an example of a region with a progressive GDP. As per the Regional Development Strategy of the Slovak Republic, the Trnava region is considered to be the most promising in terms of socio-economic development (Aktualizácia národnej stratégie, 2021, s. 78).

(3) High GDP per capita – this pertains exclusively to the Bratislava region, which is deemed to meet the socio-economic standards of Western Europe established by the EU (Aktualizácia národnej stratégie, 2021, s. 87). There is a noticeable socio-economic cleavage between the capital region and peripheral regions in the Slovak Republic, as macroeconomic data from the Bratislava region are several times higher than the national average.

1.2 Regulatory Component of Regional Elections

The Slovak Republic is divided into regions (*Kraje*), which are self-governing units with administrative and territorial responsibilities. The legal status of these regions is governed by a specialized Law "On Self-Government of Higher Territorial Units (Law on Self-Government of Regions)" which was enacted in 2001 (*"Zákon o samospráve vyšších územných celkov (zákon o samosprávnych krajoch)"*) (Zákon č. 302/2001). The degree of autonomy and overall effectiveness of self-governing regions is contingent upon their capacity to independently execute economic policies, equitably allocate profits, and ensure the fulfilment of the rights and needs of their residents (Čl.I, §1, 5) (Zákon č. 302/2001).

The Regional Assembly (*Zastupiteľstvo samosprávneho kraja*), headed by the Regional Župan (*Predseda samosprávneho kraja*) (§2, b), constitutes the representative governing body in the region. They possess extensive powers across various domains of life. Specifically, they exercise the authority to independently formulate the fundamental principles of regional policy, adopt and supervise the implementation progress of the regional budget, announce a referendum, and exert broad competence in personnel appointments of executive authorities in the region (§11, 2) (Zákon č. 302/2001).

The composition of the Regional Assemblies is determined through the electoral process, in which a specific number of officials are elected during regional elections. It is necessary to distinguish between "local elections" and "regional elections". In the context of "local elections", individuals such as local deputies, Starostas, and city Mayors were elected up until 1998. Following the establishment of the new self-governing units known as *Kraye*, the scope of local elections is now limited to the election of management staff for municipalities. The first elections for self-governing municipalities were held in the year 2002 (Voľby a referendá). In 2001, the previous system of referendá was replaced by the first elections to bodies of self-governing regions (Voľby a referendá). These regional elections are now governed by a specialized Law known as "On Elections to Bodies of Self-Governing Regions" (*"Zákon o voľbách do orgánov samosprávnych krajov"*) that was adopted in the same year. This law regulates the process of regional elections and ensures that they are conducted fairly and transparently (Zákon č. 303/2001). The legal provisions define the precise procedure for selecting deputies of Regional Assemblies through single-mandate and multi-mandate voting districts, which are created based on the population in the region (§5, 1). The establishment of a single-mandate voting district in each region is contingent upon the election of the Župan (§5, 3). The election of the Regional Assembly deputies is carried out by voting for open lists of candidates (§14, 3), with candidates from individual political parties or independent candidates being eligible to participate in the election (§14, 1) (Zákon č. 303/2001).

Regarding the candidacy for the position of Župan, there are two available options. A candidate can be nominated by a political party or can run as an independent candidate (§19, 1). The voter is permitted to choose one or more candidates from the proposed list, but it is important to note that the maximum number of candidates that can be selected should not exceed the total number of deputies from the voting district. In the case of voting for Župan, the voter is allowed to choose only one candidate (§29, 3). Upon the fulfilment of the electoral quota assigned to a particular district, the candidates who obtain the highest number of votes are duly elected as Deputies of the Regional Assemblies. In the case of the Župan elections held in 2001, it was stipulated by law that a second voting round would be conducted if no candidate received an absolute majority of votes. It is important to note that, during the second round, the majoritarian model of the relative majority is implemented (§41, §42) (Zákon č. 303/2001). The 2014 election legislation amendments have introduced a new system for electing the position of Župan. As a result, only a single-round voting process is now in place, with the rule of a relative majority of votes being the prevailing criterion (§157, 4) (Zákon č. 180/2014). In 2017, single-round elections of Župan were held for the first time (Župné voľby budú... 2017). As per the resolution put forth by the National Council, it has been decided that the forthcoming municipal and regional elections shall take place concurrently on 29 October, 2022 (Voľby do orgánov samosprávy obcí... 2022). As per the Law of 2014, local electoral processes will be held on the same day to optimize the electoral process.

The formation of voting districts in the regions is determined by the population of the respective region, as stipulated in Section 5, Clause 1, and illustrated in Table 2. It is noteworthy that one

Table 2. The Regional Assemblies Formation Principles.

Regions	Number of Inhabitants in the Region	Number of Voting Districts	Approximate Number of Deputies
Banská Bystrica region	625,601	13	49
Bratislava region	719,537	8	46
Žilina region	691,613	11	52
Košice region	782,216	11	57
Nitra region	677,900	7	52
Prešov region	808,931	13	60
Trenčín region	577,464	9	45
Trnava region	566,008	7	40
Total	5,449,270	79	401

Source: the author's calculations are based on the Law "On Elections to Bodies of Self-Governing Regions" of 2001 (Zákon č.303/2001) and the statistics obtained from the demographic census conducted for the Slovak population in 2021 (Počet obyvateľov podľa..., 2021).

deputy mandate represents an average of 12 000 to 15 000 inhabitants of the region, as per the provisions of Section 11, Clause 1 of Law 303/2001 (Zákon č. 303/2001). These figures are not absolute, but rather indicative, and ensure that the interests of a reasonably equal number of residents of the region are represented by one deputy.

To implement the decentralization reform, legislation was enacted on 4 July, 2001, to regulate electoral processes in the regions. The legal framework comprised the Law "On Self-Government of Higher Territorial Units (Law on Self-Government of Regions)" and the Law "On Elections to Bodies of Self-Governing Regions". According to section 23, paragraph 4, the elections are scheduled for a single Saturday, between 7:00 a.m. and 10:00 p.m. (Zákon č.303/2001). Both citizens of the Slovak Republic and foreign residents who possess the status of "permanent residence" are entitled to exercise their right to vote in regional elections[2] (§7, 1) (Zákon č. 303/2001). The current situation regarding the tenure of the deputies of the Regional Assembly and Župans presents an interesting case. The duration of their term in office is four years each. However, to streamline the electoral process and reduce election expenses, the parliament of the country decided to conduct regional and local elections simultaneously. By the decision of the National Council of the Slovak Republic, the last elections for the Regional Assemblies, local councils, and Župans were held on Saturday, 29 October, 2022 (Voľby do orgánov samosprávy obcí..., 2022).

In light of the electoral reform that took place in Slovakia in 2014, several changes were made to the term of office for deputies of Regional Assemblies. Specifically, the term was extended to five years, which was enshrined in the Law "On Conditions for Exercising the Right to Vote" ("Zákon o podmienkach výkonu volebného práva") (Zákon č. 180/2014). The current issues that Slovakia faces have significantly impacted changes in electoral legislation. For instance, the COVID-19 pandemic directly influenced the adoption of the Law "On a Special Method of Voting" ("Zákon o špeciálnom spôsobe hlasovania vo voľbách do orgánov samosprávy obcí a vo

---

2 A certificate of "permanent residence" is issued in the Slovak Republic to foreigners who meet the current requirements for five years, with the possibility of extension (Trvalý pobyt..., 2024).

voľbách do orgánov samosprávnych krajov") (Zákon č. 185/2022) for the elections to the Regional Assemblies and local councils in October 2022, which occurred at the end of May 2022. The regional and local elections in the autumn of 2022 were of considerable importance to Slovakia, as they occurred amidst the coronavirus pandemic and the stringent quarantine measures enforced by the government. These elections were expected to hold significant symbolic value for the modern Slovak Republic.

1.3 Election Turnout: National, Local, European, and Regional Levels

The interest of voters in electing representatives to a specific authority or official provides a comprehensive insight into the political priorities of a nation. As the Slovak Republic gradually distances itself from its socialist past and transitions towards political pluralism, the priorities of Slovak voters are also beginning to take shape. An examination of electoral turnout over several decades since the country's independence reveals a clear preponderance of national-level politics. The highest voter turnout is observed in parliamentary and presidential elections in the modern Slovak Republic.

In Slovakia's modern political landscape, there have been 11 election campaigns for the National Council since the emergence of political pluralism. The highest electoral indicator recorded in the country is an average voter turnout of 70.51%. Despite each election having its own unique political history, societal crises, and significant political confrontations, it is evident that voter turnout increases during times of systemic change in the country:

- in 1990, Slovaks expressed their firm support towards the anti-communist reforms and a shift away from the "socialist model of government";
- during the 1992 elections in Czechoslovakia, one of the pivotal issues was the future format of the state model and the endorsement of the "course for independence" advocated by Slovak conservatives;

- in 1998, Slovakia was deeply entrenched in a political stand-off between two opposing forces, such as a populist leader Vladimír Mečiar and a pro-European coalition led by Mikuláš Dzurinda (Haydanka, 2021a);
- ultimately, in recent elections, there has been an increase in voter turnout, which has reversed the trend of low turnout from 2006 to 2016. This was made possible by the crisis in Robert Fico's government, as well as the desire for "new faces" in politics (in the end, populist Igor Matovič became such a "face"). However, despite this state of affairs, Robert Fico was able to return to the prime minister's chair in the 2023 early parliamentary elections.

The Slovak Republic has held six presidential elections to date, with the first national direct voting being implemented in 1999. The average turnout for these elections has been recorded as 52.46%. It is noteworthy that the 1999 presidential election recorded an unusually high turnout of 74.67%, which is indicative of the intense competition between the Mečiar camp and the anti-Mečiar political factions. It is also pertinent that the 1999 presidential election was the second most popular election in terms of electoral popularity. Between 2004 and 2014, presidential elections in Slovakia did not generate much interest among voters. These included Vladimír Mečiar's attempt to regain power through the presidency in 2004, Ivan Gašparovič's second term in 2009, and the victory of independent candidate Andrej Kiska in 2014. Throughout this decade, the turnout for these elections ranged between 45% and 47% (Voľby a referendá). According to official records, the presidential election held in 2019 witnessed a voter turnout of less than 50%, with an average of 45.26% after both rounds were completed. Despite the relatively low participation rate, Zuzana Čaputová, the first female President of the Slovak Republic, emerged victorious and celebrated a historic win (Voľby a referendá). In post-socialist countries, female politicians rarely achieve victory in presidential elections due to a prevalent conservatism and distrust towards women in politics. Nonetheless, in 2019, Zuzana Čaputová managed to establish herself as a new and influential figure in Slovak politics. This occurred during a time of deep political crisis, and her success was largely attributed to her ability to create a favourable political image for herself (Haydanka, 2021b, p. 43). In the

2024 presidential election, the voter turnout exceeded 50%. To be precise, 51.91% of eligible voters participated in the first round, and 61.14% in the second round (Voľby a referendá). The numbers show a tight race between the pro-Fico candidate Peter Pellegrini and the opposition candidate Ivan Korčok. The victory of the former was primarily a win for Robert Fico, who regained control of the presidential power (Csanyi, 2024, p. 7). During 2023–2024, Robert Fico's political revenge gradually unfolded in the Slovak Republic.

The local elections in Slovakia are known to generate a significant level of interest among eligible voters, with an average turnout of 48.34% (Voľby a referendá). This high percentage corresponds to the number of people who vote in presidential elections, except for the first popular vote for the President in 1999, which was a milestone in Slovakia's political system. The most recent local elections were held jointly with regional elections in October 2022, and the voter turnout remained practically the same – slightly over 46% (Voľby a referendá). Undoubtedly, such a high turnout rate in local elections confirms the significant interest of Slovak voters in addressing local problems.

The European Parliament elections in Slovakia have experienced a low turnout of voters. This is attributed to a combination of endogenous and exogenous factors (Gyárfášová & Henderson, 2018). The introduction of the EU elections in 2004 was a significant milestone for the Slovak electorate. From 2004 until the occurrence of Brexit in January 2020, the Slovak Republic had delegated 13 members to the European Parliament (and 14 members in Elections 2019). Presently, the European Parliament has a total of 705 seats, and Slovakia has been allocated 15 seats[3] (Európske voľby, 2024). Five rounds of European election campaigns were conducted, and the average voter turnout of 21.35% implies that Slovaks are less inclined towards European politics. The recent European elections witnessed a significant surge in voter turnout, setting a new record for the Slovak Republic. Notably, 34% of eligible voters participated, underscoring the growing role of European poli-

---

3 For comparison, Ireland (14 deputies), Croatia (12), Lithuania (11), Latvia and Slovenia (9 deputies each), Estonia (7), Cyprus, Luxembourg, and Malta (6 deputies) delegate fewer deputies to the European Parliament than Slovakia (Infographic..., 2024).

tics. This increase in voter engagement was observed across all
EU member states. One contributing factor to the heightened interest in European politics among Slovak voters is the concurrent
scheduling of EU elections with parliamentary and presidential
elections (Fauvelle-Aymar & Stegmaier, 2008). It is worth noting
the heightened electoral engagement of Slovak youth with a "European mindset", who attained the right to vote in 2024 (Survey...,
2019). However, it is noteworthy that these elections are typically
classified as "Second-order Elections" (Kovář, 2016). The electoral
turnout of Slovaks was the lowest among all member states of the
EU during the 2004–2019 election campaigns. However, the 2019
elections witnessed an almost 23% voter turnout, which slightly improved the overall situation. The outcome of the recent European
elections in 2024 has brought significant changes. As a result, the
Slovak Republic, while not attaining a leading position, has tran-
sitioned from its long-standing last place (Turnout by year, 2024).

The overall state of election turnout in the modern period of the
development of democracy in the Slovak Republic directly affects
the electoral preferences of Slovaks and is presented in Table 3.

The voter turnout in regional elections is notably lower than
that of national elections, such as those for the President and Parliament. The only elections that exhibit lower turnout are the European elections, in which Slovak voters demonstrate a compara-
tively low interest. Nonetheless, resolving local issues through local
elections garners higher interest within the Slovak Republic. Two
major characteristics define voter turnout in regional elections.

Firstly, upon analysing the data on Slovak electoral activity in
regional elections, it is possible to identify the highest and lowest
turnouts. Of note, there was the lowest turnout in 2005, with only
slightly over 18% of eligible voters exercising their right to elect
the regional elite (Voľby a referendá). The electoral landscape of
2004–2005 revealed a certain weariness among Slovak voters. At
the start of 2004, Slovaks were tasked with deciding their European
future and supporting the country's accession to the EU. Additionally, the country's President was elected for a second term through
direct voting. Furthermore, in June 2004, Slovaks were awaiting
their first opportunity to vote in the European Parliament elections. The parliamentary elections of 2002 were of significant importance as the nation required a government that prioritized Eu-

Table 3. Election Turnout in the Slovak Republic (1990–2024).

Election Type	Year and Percentage										
Parliamentary[4]	**1990**	**1992**	**1994**	**1998**	**2002**	**2006**	**2010**	**2012**	**2016**	**2020**	**2023**
	95.39	84.20	75.65	84.24	70.06	54.67	58.83	59.11	59.82	65.80	68.51
Presidential[5]	**1999**	**2004**	**2009**	**2014**	**2019**	**2024**					
	74.67	45.72	47.65	46.94	45.26	56.52					
Local[6]	**2002**	**2006**	**2010**	**2014**	**2018**	**2022**[7]					
	49.51	47.65	49.69	48.34	48.67	46.19					
Regional[8]	**2001**	**2005**	**2009**	**2013**	**2017**	**2022**					
	26.02	18.02	22.90	20.11	29.95	43.74					
Euroelections	**2004**	**2009**	**2014**	**2019**	**2024**						
	16.96	19.64	13.05	22.74	34.38						

Source: author's calculations based on the Statistical Office of the Slovak Republic (Voľby a referendá).

ropean integration. The regional elections of 2005 witnessed a low turnout, which could be attributed to voter exhaustion resulting from the overlapping of various elections. The most recent election in 2022 had the highest turnout of 43.74% (Voľby a referendá). These are the outcomes of the municipal and regional elections conducted jointly.

In terms of regional elections, there appears to be a consistent turnout across all regions, with no noticeable variations (see Table 4).

However, the Banská Bystrica region in central Slovakia stands out with the highest turnout rate exceeding 40% in 2017. This is the only region with such a high turnout rate at the Regional Assembly election. It is worth noting that this analysis excludes the results of the joint elections in 2022. The regional policy for Slovakia's two regional poles, Bratislava and Košice, is of limited interest to the electorate, as evidenced by a voter turnout of less than one-quarter in regional elections.

---

4 The first two competitive parliamentary elections (1990 and 1992) were held in the Czechoslovak Federation's state format.
5 The average indicator for the first and second rounds of voting is displayed.
6 The local elections that occurred after the implementation of the decentralization reform are considered.
7 On 29 October, 2022, the Župans elections were held concurrently with the Regional Assemblies and municipal authorities' elections.
8 When there are two rounds of voting in an election, only the results of the first round are shown.

Table 4. Voter Turnout in the Elections for the Regional Assemblies in the Slovak Republic (2001–2022 percentages)[9].

Regions	2001	2005	2009	2013	2017	2022	B
Bratislava region	23.96	14.45	19.46	21.65	31.34	38.60	24.91
Trnava region	33.73	14.50	20.46	17.46	24.74	42.87	25.62
Nitra region	34.69	27.67	21.81	17.90	26.83	43.10	28.66
Trenčín region	21.55	12.30	20.59	17.37	26.32	44.80	23.82
Žilina region	23.47	15.69	23.68	21.57	33.84	48.74	27.83
Banská Bystrica region	24.16	18.65	27.06	24.59	40.29	45.13	29.98
Košice region	21.79	19.27	22.93	17.77	26.73	39.70	24.69
Prešov region	25.50	19.47	26.31	22.13	29.40	47.50	28.38
A	26.02	18.05	22.90	20.11	29.95	43.74	

A - average voter turnout by year of regional elections; **B** - average voter turnout in the regions
Source: author's calculations based on the Statistical Office of the Slovak Republic (Voľby a referendá).

---

9 The results of the first round of voting are displayed.

2 Political Fragmentation of the Slovak Republic in the Context of Regional Elections (2001–2017)

2.1 2001 Elections

The first regional elections in the Slovak Republic became a significant milestone in formalizing regional electoral processes. They also served as a litmus test for the electorate's capacity to select regional representatives. The 2001 Slovak regional elections were conducted amidst a backdrop of political uncertainty. Notably, they coincided with the transfer of power from the prominent post-communist figure of the 1990s, Vladimír Mečiar, to a broad anti-Mečiar coalition with a strong focus on integrating with Western Europe. Following the significant 1998 parliamentary elections in Slovakia, the country witnessed a power transfer. Despite the victory in the elections[10], Vladimír Mečiar's HZDS Party lost control of the government. The newly established government, under the leadership of Mikuláš Dzurinda, relied on an unstable, multi-ideological parliamentary majority, primarily composed of SDK and SDĽ deputies. However, Mečiar's political forces and individual politicians continued to maintain substantial political influence in the regions. This set the stage for the second significant political aspect of the 2001 regional elections: the potential for regional elites loyal to Vladimír Mečiar to assume control of the regions. On one hand, regional governments in opposition to the central government remained a formidable tool for HZDS's political influence. On the other hand, the prevalence of Mečiar's forces at the regional level raised the likelihood of HZDS's political resurgence in the forthcoming 2002 parliamentary elections.

The inaugural regional elections were made possible through a political compromise among various political entities during the decentralization reform in the Slovak Republic. Following the dissolution of the socialist Czechoslovak federation in 1990, the issue of further administrative and territorial organization remained unresolved. The formation of the Czech and Slovak Republics in 1992 intensified the necessity for efficient administrative and territorial reform. The period spanning the mid-1990s to the early

---

10 HZDS managed to surpass its main opponent SDK, but the difference in electoral support was only 0.67% – HZDS had 27% compared to SDK's 26.33% (Voľby a referendá).

2000s in the Slovak Republic witnessed a tense political choice between centralization and regionalization. This debate featured the prominent figure of the centralism proponent Vladimír Mečiar and a cohort of Slovak politicians seeking to establish an optimal model of decentralization for the country. Notably, Viktor Nižňanský emerged as a pivotal figure or the "godfather" in championing and implementing the decentralization reform within the framework of the government of Mikuláš Dzurinda (Nižňanský, Cibáková, & Hamalová, 2014). Furthermore, the initiation of the inaugural regional elections in 2001 represented a significant milestone in the context of political decentralization. It was imperative to bestow upon the newly elected regional authorities the autonomy to govern themselves, including the administration of independent financial and budgetary policies.

The process of "Europeanization" and the incorporation of the concept of "subsidiarity" into the public administration system were pivotal elements in the regionalization of Slovak politics (Brusis, 2008, p. 103–104). The first regional elections in the Slovak Republic garnered a favourable evaluation from Council of Europe observers, indicating a significant achievement. The report underscored the "free" and "democratic" nature of the elections. Nonetheless, the limited voter turnout could be attributed to the population's insufficient awareness of the elections (Haas, 2001). The ultimate phase of decentralization, encompassing the reform of fiscal decentralization in the regions, was successfully concluded in 2004, aligning with the Slovak Republic's accession to the EU (Nižňanský, Cibáková, & Hamalová, 2014). The Slovak regions were able to successfully access EU financial funds, thereby contributing to the stimulation of regional policy development.

The first regional elections in the Slovak Republic were originally set for 1 December but were ultimately held in two rounds, with seven out of eight Župans elected during the second round on 15 December (2001 – Voľby do orgánov). The regional elections transpired amidst a political contest between Mečiar's HZDS and its primary rivals such as SDKÚ-DS and ANO, among others. However, discernible discrepancies in the electoral landscape were noted at the regional level. Electoral coalitions emerged within the regions, incorporating ideologically contrasting political entities.

These coalitions frequently coalesced to counter Mečiar's HZDS. Notably, in the Bratislava region, a coalition of five political forces was established with the shared objective of opposing Mečiar[11]. The election results revealed that the anti-Mečiar coalition secured 40 out of 46 available seats in the Bratislava Regional Assembly. Notably, the coalition's candidate, Ľubomír Roman, claimed victory for the post of Župan in the first round, departing from the typical practice in Slovakian regional elections. Furthermore, it is worth highlighting the exceptional performance of HZDS, as they obtained all 45 available seats in the Trenčín region.

Additionally, independent candidates have begun to wield influence in regional elections. This was evident in Slovakia's electoral processes, with the exception of the first national presidential elections in 1999. Independent candidates only secured 4.48% of deputy seats in the Regional Assemblies (18 out of 401 possible mandates). Subsequent regional elections have highlighted the potential of independent candidates as an alternative to traditional political ideologies. However, scholars studying Slovakia's electoral processes have frequently questioned the level of candidates' "independence" from major political parties (Martinkovič, 2018).

One of the significant features of the regional elections in the Slovak Republic was the presence of a Hungarian minority. The leading party representing the Hungarian minority in Slovakia, SMK-MKP, achieved one of the best results by winning 60 out of 401 seats as a separate political force. The party received strong support in regions with a considerable Hungarian ethnic minority population, such as Nitra, Trnava, and Banská Bystrica. Additionally, SMK-MKP successfully participated in pre-election coalitions, particularly in the five-subject coalition in the Bratislava region, contributing to their success. Since the early 1990s, the Hungarian ethnic minority has played a significant role in influencing the electoral behaviour of the residents in the southern and northern regions of the Slovak Republic (Krivý, Feglová, & Balko, 1998).

---

11 Coalition: ANO, DS, KDH, SDKÚ, SMK–MKP.

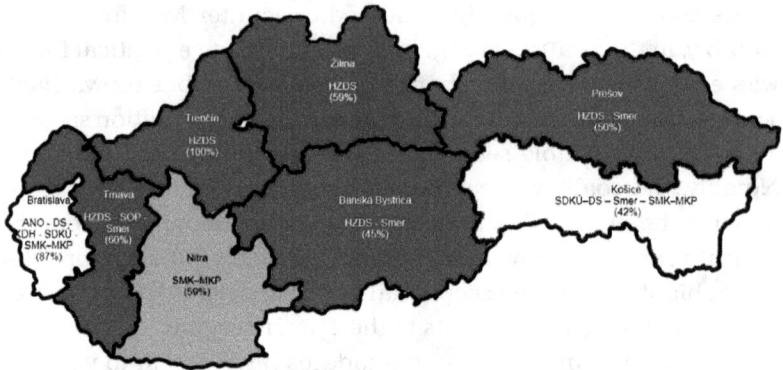

Figure 2. Electoral Map of the Slovak Regions According to the 2001 Regional Elections[12].

Source: the author's calculations are based on the Statistical Office of the Slovak Republic (Voľby a referendá)

In the 2001 regional elections, the HZDS Party emerged as the leading winner, securing nearly half of the deputy seats in the Regional Assemblies, with a representation of 47.6%. The party independently nominated candidates in certain regions, such as Trenčín and Žilina, and also formed electoral coalitions. Notably, the social democrats Smer frequently aligned with HZDS in these coalitions, and later played a pivotal role in the political landscape of the Slovak Republic. The pro-government party SDKÚ demonstrated modest performance in the elections. SDKÚ attained the highest number of seats solely through electoral coalitions, which included traditional centre-right parties (KDH, DS), newly formed liberal forces (ANO), and the party representing the Hungarian minority (SMK-MKP). Notably, this electoral coalition achieved significant success in the Bratislava region, securing a victory by a large margin. The political dichotomy of "Mečiarism" versus "anti-Mečiarism" (Haughton, 2003) shifted from the national to the regional level. The KDH christian democrats garnered support in the eastern (Prešov) and northern (Žilina) regions in the initial re-

12 The winners (independent candidates or political forces) in the regions are given. In each region, the electoral outcome of the political party or electoral coalition that secured the highest number of mandates in the Regional Assembly is indicated. Electoral data is presented as a percentage of the received mandates from the entire composition of the Regional Assembly.

gional elections. Notably, independent candidates exhibited promising performance, particularly in the eastern areas of Prešov and Košice.

According to the results of the initial regional elections, several groups of Slovak regions can be distinguished:

(1) Electorally homogeneous regions denote areas where a single political force or electoral bloc overwhelmingly dominates, securing an absolute majority of seats. For instance, in the Trenčín region, the HDZS Party claimed all 45 seats in the Regional Assembly, creating an exceptional case with minimal political competition during the initial regional elections. Other instances include the Bratislava region, where the anti-Mečiar coalition achieved 87% of the seats (40 out of 46), the Trnava region, where the HZDS-led coalition garnered 60% of the seats (24 out of 40), and both the Nitra and Žilina regions, where two parties secured similar results, with an electoral advantage of 59% or 31 mandates out of 52 possible. In the former case, the SMK-MKP Hungarian party was successful, while in the latter, it was the HZDS Party. The Prešov region illustrated the lowest level of electoral homogeneity, with half of seats (30 out of 60) secured by a two-party coalition consisting of HZDS-Smer.

(2) Electorally heterogeneous regions are those characterized by electoral diversity, with no single political force able to secure the majority of seats in the Regional Assembly. The 2001 election results demonstrate that only two regions, Banská Bystrica and Košice, fell into this category. In the Banská Bystrica region, the primary competition was among three political forces: the HZDS-Smer coalition (obtaining 22 out of 49 seats), the Hungarian minority party SMK-MKP (securing 15 seats), and the centre-right four-party coalition ANO-DS-KDH-SDKÚ, which garnered seven seats, marginally behind the other two competitors. In the Košice region, the contest for power involved four forces: the anti-Mečiar coalition comprising SDKÚ-Smer-SMK-MKP (securing 24 out of 57 seats), the Mečiar coalition HZDS-SOP-SDĽ (with 14 seats), another group of anti-Mečiar forces ANO-DS-KDH (with 10 seats), and a group of independent candidates (with 8 seats).

Two weeks after the first round, the subsequent round of regional elections was conducted (see Table 5).

Table 5. Župans Elected in the Regions of the Slovak Republic (according to the results of the 2001 regional elections).

Župan	Region	Election Round	Party/Electoral Coalition	Votes (%)
Ľubomír Roman	Bratislava	1	SDKÚ-**KDH**-ANO-SMK-MKP-DS[6]	56.49
Peter Tomeček	Trnava	2	**HZDS**-Smer-SOP	61.48
Štefan Štefanec	Trenčín	2	**HZDS**	67.92
Milan Belica	Nitra	2	**HZDS**-SDĽ-STRED-SOP	61.37
Jozef Tarčák	Žilina	2	**HZDS**	80.31
Milan Marčok	Banská Bystrica	2	**HZDS**-Smer	52.36
Peter Chudík	Prešov	2	**HZDS**-Smer	50.11
Rudolf Bauer	Košice	2	**KDH**-DS	59.38

Source: the author's calculations are based on the Statistical Office of the Slovak Republic (Voľby a referendá).

The second round concerns only the election of Župans. In accordance with the regional election regulations, the two candidates who received the highest number of votes have progressed to the second round. However, none of the candidates managed to secure an absolute majority, defined as more than 50% of the votes (§41, 4; §42, 1–2) (Zákon č. 303/2001). Only the Bratislava Region managed to elect a Župan in the first round. Ľubomír Roman, who was nominated by a broad anti-Mečiar coalition, although he directly represented the KDH, could potentially fulfil this role. Ľubomír Roman had prior political experience as a minister and a deputy in the National Council of the Slovak Republic (Zomrel herec..., 2022). Ľubomír Roman garnered the support of 56.49% of voters, while HZDS candidate Milan Čič secured 32.97% of the votes. Importantly, the Bratislava region successfully elected its first Župan with a strong level of legitimacy and public approval, in the first round of elections.

In the remaining seven regions, the Župan was elected only in the second round of voting. The least political struggle was ob-

---

13 The newly elected Župan is a member of the party highlighted in bold.

served in the Žilina region, where HZDS representative, Jozef
Tarčák, secured victory with 80.31% of the votes in the second
round. Prior to the regional elections, Jozef Tarčák had gained extensive experience through three parliamentary terms in the National Council as a member of the political forces associated with
Mečiar (Tarčák, 2024). The elected Župans in the Trnava, Trenčín,
Nitra, and Košice regions garnered significant electoral support,
ranging from 1.5 to 2 times the anticipated levels. Peter Tomeček,
a candidate representing HZDS–Smer–SOP, secured the position
of Župan in the Trnava region with 61.48% of the vote. Although
associated with HZDS, he was not widely recognized for notable
political accomplishments before or after assuming the role of
Župan. In the Trenčín region, HZDS member Štefan Štefanec
claimed victory with 67.92% of the vote. Prior to assuming the position of Župan, Štefanec was a relatively well-known local politician
and had previously served as mayor of the city of Dubnica nad
Váhom (Životopis, 2001). Milan Belica commenced his long-term
career as a Župan in the Nitra region. During the elections, he
was the representative for HZDS and secured victory against his
opponent Miklós Fehér from the Hungarian party SMK-MKP with
61.37% of the vote. Meanwhile, in the Košice region, Rudolf Bauer
from KDH emerged triumphant with 59.38% of the votes. Rudolf
Bauer, an experienced local politician, had previously served as
mayor of Košice in the early 1990s and later as a member of the
National Council. Following his tenure as Župan of the Košice region, he was elected as a member of the parliament (Bauer, 2024).

In another two regions, the competition for the position of
Župan was notably intense, with both candidates demonstrating
similar results in the second round. Notably, in the Banská Bystrica region, Milan Marčok from the HZDS–Smer coalition attained the position of Župan with a 52.36% majority vote. Milan
Marčok is esteemed as an academic professor and has previously
served as the rector at the Technical University in Zvolen (Nový
rektor..., 2001). The extent of his political experience is limited
to the position of Župan. The candidates closest to securing the
Župan position in the second round received substantial support
in the Prešov region. Peter Chudík, representing the coalition
HZDS–Smer, secured victory over the SDKÚ-KDH opponent with
a narrow margin of 0.23% (Chudík's result was 50.11%). This suc-

cess marked Chudík's first term as the long-standing Župan of the Prešov region, following his victory in the subsequent elections.

2.2 2005 Elections

The regional elections in the Slovak Republic were conducted at the end of November 2005. The first round took place on 26 November, 2005, and was followed by the second round on 10 December, 2005, two weeks later (2005 – Voľby do orgánov). These elections recorded the lowest voter turnout compared to subsequent election campaigns. During the first round, the turnout was 18%, and in the second round, only 11% of voters came to elect Župans. One of the primary reasons for the low turnout of Slovaks in the regional elections was voter fatigue, for Slovaks had to participate in the 2004 presidential election and the first-ever elections to the European Parliament. Furthermore, it is pertinent to mention the May 2003 referendum on the accession of the Slovak Republic to the EU, which saw a turnout exceeding the required 50% (2003 – Účasť oprávnených občanov). It is important to acknowledge another factor contributing to the significantly low voter turnout in the second round of regional elections in Slovakia. Commencing from December, the Christmas holidays in the Slovak Republic make it challenging to secure involvement in any elections scheduled towards the latter half of the month.

The regional elections were closely entwined with national political dynamics. By the end of 2005, the political landscape of the Slovak Republic had attained a relative state of stability. Mikuláš Dzurinda continued to serve as the Prime Minister, heading a government established on an unstable yet operative coalition led by the modernized SDKÚ. The principal objective of Dzurinda's second government was accomplished, with the nation's accession to the EU in May 2004. Meanwhile, within the sphere of political parties, the emergent influence of the future long-term Prime Minister, Robert Fico from SMER, started to grow. Established in 1999 as a political alternative to the populist conservatives HZSD and the pro-European SDK (SMER-SD, 2024), the party earned recognition as the "third force" in Slovak politics. The parliamentary elections subsequently validated this status, with SMER securing third place, trailing behind HZSD and SDKÚ (2002 – Voľby do NR SR). The 2005 regional elections tested SMER's political maturity and showcased their search for regional political support in anticipation of the 2006 parliamentary elections.

The 2005 regional elections held in the year subsequent to the Slovak Republic's accession to the EU retained the traditional electoral cleavages that significantly influenced the voting patterns of Slovaks. In particular, the enduring impact of the "centre–periphery" and "west–east" cleavages on voter behaviour was notable (Szabó & Tátrai, 2016, p. 195). The potential electoral interference in elections by a new influential player, SMER, could have reshaped the traditional electoral cleavages between regions. In 2005, a larger number of members were elected to the Regional Assemblies compared to the first elections in 2001, resulting in 11 more seats and a total of 412 deputies to be elected. Notably, the number of regional deputies increased in the metropolitan Bratislava region (+4 seats), Žilina region (+5), and Prešov region (+2). While the increase in the number of mandates did not significantly impact the political struggle, it served as a significant statistical indicator, which influenced subsequent regional elections. Additionally, the 2005 regional elections saw the most successful candidates emerging from the coalition electoral unions. The most prominent political forces, including ĽS-HZDS, KDH, and SDKÚ, were actively seeking coalition partners to secure a majority in the Regional Assembly. Notably, in the Nitra region, parliamentary seats were distributed between two main forces: the historically influential party representing the Hungarian minority, SMK-MKP, and a broad coalition of five parties representing diverse political ideologies[14].

The third feature of the 2005 regional elections was a significant shift in the key political actors vying for seats in the Regional Assemblies. The performance of the pro-government SDKÚ was not particularly noteworthy, primarily due to its participation in

---

14 The electoral coalition included the Christian Democrats (KDH), Mečiar's populists (ĽS-HZDS), the pro-government centre-right party (SDKÚ), the right-wing nationalists (SNS), and the social democrats (SMER-SD).

electoral coalitions where it was far from being a headliner. The centre-right coalitions, particularly those involving the KDH, emerged as the most effective. Conversely, their chief opponents, ĽS-HZDS did not attain widespread success and once again entered ideologically diverse electoral coalitions, despite having secured votes in their traditional strongholds such as the Trenčín and Banská Bystrica regions. The KDH Christian Democrats secured a commendable number of votes, and electoral coalitions involving them emerged as frontrunners in most regions. Additionally, Robert Fico's SMER-SD project was gaining significant electoral momentum, capturing the electoral niche of the social democratic party in the central and eastern regions of the country. The elections also featured some unexpected participants, including the moderately successful political project HZD, established in 2002 by the future President of the Slovak Republic Ivan Gašparovič, closely associated with Vladimír Mečiar (Gašparovič založil..., 2002). SMER-SD emerged as their principal coalition partner and achieved notable success in their collaboration.

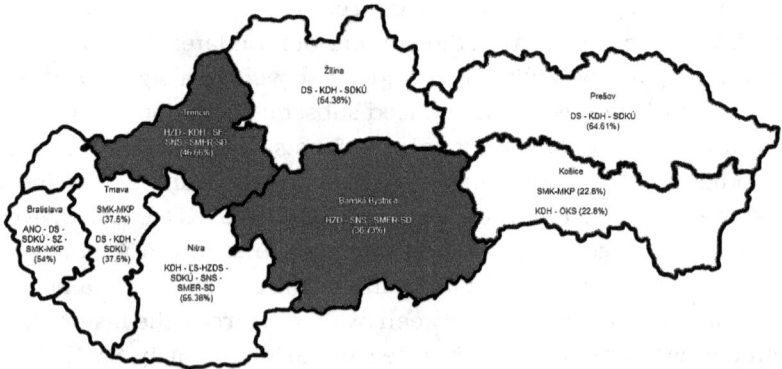

Figure 3. Electoral Map of the Slovak Regions According to the 2005 Regional Elections[15].

Source: the author's calculations are based on the Statistical Office of the Slovak Republic (Voľby a referendá).

15 The winners (independent candidates or political forces) in the regions are given. In each region, the electoral outcome of the political party or electoral coalition that secured the highest number of seats in the Regional Assembly is indicated. The electoral data is represented as a percentage of the received mandates from the entire composition of the Regional Assembly.

The 2005 regional elections resulted in the division of the regions of the Slovak Republic into two groups:

(1) Electorally homogeneous regions refer to regions where
a specific electoral coalition received the majority of mandates
for the Regional Assembly. In the Bratislava region, a centre-right
coalition consisting of five parties won, receiving 54% of the seats
(27 out of 50 parliamentary seats). The Žilina region saw 54.38% of
all mandates (31 parliamentary seats out of 57 possible) won by
a centre-right three-party electoral coalition supporting the policy
of the Mikuláš Dzurinda government. In the Prešov region, the
pro-government coalition, led by KDH, also emerged as the winner, which was perhaps a little unexpected. The coalition achieved
a better result than in the north of the country (Žilina region), winning 64.51% of all the seats in the Assembly (40 out of 62). However,
the highest level of dominance was seen in the Nitra region. In
this south Slovak region, where a significant Hungarian minority
resides, all major political forces with different ideologies joined
together to oppose the SMK-MKP. As a result, a coalition of five
parties, including ĽS-HZDS and SDKÚ, won 65.38% of the seats in
the regional representative office (34 out of 52). In comparison,
their main rivals, SMK-MKP alone, only received 32.69% of the
mandates (17 seats in the Assembly).

(2) In electorally heterogeneous regions (regions with diverse
voting patterns), no single political party traditionally wins a majority of seats in the Regional Assembly. This dynamic is observed
in four other regions of the Slovak Republic. The most intense
competition was seen in the Košice region, where eight political
parties and a group of independent deputies secured seats in the
Assembly. The most powerful were SMK-MKP (22.8% of all seats),
the centre-right coalition of KDH–OKS (also 22.8% of seats), and
the conservative coalition HZD–SMER-SD (21.05% of seats). The
Trnava and Trenčín regions also experienced close electoral contests, with two main political forces vying for seats in the Regional
Assembly. In Trnava, the party representing the Hungarian minority, SMK-MKP, and the centre-right coalition led by KDH[16] both secured 15 out of 40 possible seats (37.5% of seats each). In the Trenčín
region, the main struggle took place between two closely aligned

---

16 Coalition members: DS, KDH, SDKÚ.

electoral coalitions. One coalition was made up of ĽS-HZDS and the other included HZD with SMER-SD. The latter emerged victorious, securing 46.66% of the deputies' mandates, while their rivals conceded with 44.44%. In the Banská Bystrica region, the conservative coalition of HZD, SNS, and SMER-SD secured 36.73% of mandates. Additionally, three other political forces received almost equal support: the party of Hungarians SMK-MKP with 16.32% of mandates, and the coalitions with KDH and ĽS-HZDS, each receiving 18.36% of the deputies.

Notably, 9.46% of mandates (or 39 out of 412 deputy seats) in the Regional Assemblies were won by independent candidates. So far, independent candidates have not been able to significantly challenge traditional party ideologies. However, one in every ten deputy seats was filled by an independent candidate, which is a positive trend. The regional elections of 2005 mirrored the electoral trends observed in the 2001 elections, characterized by low voter turnout, a focus on electoral coalitions, and limited participation of female candidates (Benkovičová, 2006).

In the 2005 regional elections, all Župans were elected only in the second round (see Table 6). The second round of voting took place on 10 December, with a voter turnout of only 11.07%.

In the metropolitan Bratislava region, independent candidate Vladimír Bajan secured a decisive victory with 67.39% of the support, giving him a two-fold advantage over his main competitor, the former Župan Ľubomír Roman. Notably, Bajan became the first Župan elected as an independent candidate. This marked a significant milestone in the political landscape of the capital, considering Bajan's extensive experience as a head of Petržalka, one of the largest urban areas of the city (Starosta Petržalky..., 2018). In the Nitra region, there was no political contest for the position of Župan, either. The previous Župan, Milan Belica, secured a resounding victory representing a broad conservative coalition with ĽS-HZDS. Milan Belica won with an overwhelming 74.08% of the vote.

In other regions, a notable contest unfolded during the second round of voting. For instance, in the western part of the country, Tibor Mikuš secured his position as Župan for the first time in the Trnava region, receiving 54.74% of the votes. He represented the populist conservative ĽS-HZDS and is renowned as one of the most prominent regional politicians in the Slovak Republic. While Mikuš

Table 6. Župans Elected in the Regions of the Slovak Republic (according to the results of the 2005 regional elections).

Župan	Region	Voting Round	Party/Electoral Coalition	Votes (%)
Vladimír Bajan	Bratislava	2	Independent	67.39
Tibor Mikuš	Trnava	2	ĽB-**ĽS-HZDS**-SNS-ZSNS[17]	54.74
Pavol Sedláček	Trenčín	2	ANO-**ĽS-HZDS**-SNS-ZSNS	51.83
Milan Belica[18]	Nitra	2	ASV-KSS-ĽB-**ĽS-HZDS**-SNS-ZSNS	74.08
Juraj Blanár	Žilina	2	ANO-HZD-SNS-**SMER**	51.37
Milan Murgaš	Banská Bystrica	2	HZD-KDH-SNS-**SMER**-SZS	50.88
Peter Chudík	Prešov	2	HZD-SNS-**SMER**	53.03
Zdenko Trebuľa	Košice	2	HZD-**SMER**	57.52

Source: the author's calculations are based on the Statistical Office of the Slovak Republic (Voľby a referendá).

has been elected to the National Council of the Slovak Republic twice under the ĽS-HZDS, he is most notably recognized for his role as the Župan of the Trnava region (Tibor Mikuš..., 2016). Pavol Sedláček, another representative of the ĽS-HZDS, secured victory in the Trenčín region by a narrow margin, obtaining 51.83% of the votes. Throughout his political career, he primarily focused on engaging in communal and regional politics within the Trenčín region (Zomrel bývalý..., 2015). In the Žilina region, Juraj Blanár, a member of SMER-SD, secured victory with 51.37% of the votes. Blanár is a widely recognized Slovak politician who has held ministerial positions and has been elected to the National Council from SMER-SD on multiple occasions (Blanár..., 2024). Milan Murgaš, another member of SMER-SD in the Banská Bystrica region with a slight advantage, received support from 50.88% of the voters. In 2002, he was elected to the National Council of the Slovak Republic. Murgaš is also known for holding high administrative positions in higher education, including serving as rector at Matej Bel University in Banská Bystrica (SME reports..., 2012). The race for the position

---

17 The newly elected Župan is a member of the party highlighted in bold.
18 Župans who were re-elected are highlighted in italics.

of Župan in the Prešov region was very close, with Peter Chudík (53.03%), affiliated with SMER-SD, managing to secure the position for the second consecutive time. This extended Chudík's tenure, preparing for two more upcoming terms. In the Košice region, the former mayor of Košice, Zdenko Trebuľa, won (57.92%).

2.3 2009 Elections

The regular elections for the Regional Assemblies were held earlier than usual, taking place in two rounds on 14 November and 28 November, 2009 (2009 – Voľby do orgánov). The regional elections were shifted to an earlier date in order to avoid overlapping with the Christmas-New Year period. This shift impacted the entire election cycle. In the 2009 regional elections, there was a turnout of 22.9%, which was almost 5% higher than the 2005 turnout of 18.02%. One contributing factor to the increased turnout was that only half of the regions elected their Župans in the second round. The rise in voter participation in the first round also boosted the legitimacy of the Regional Assemblies and their leaders (Župans).

In 2009, the regional elections in Slovakia marked the beginning of Robert Fico's political era at the national level. This period saw the transition from the "Mečiarism–anti-Mečiarism" bipolar struggle to the political dominance of the SMER-SD Party. In 2006, Robert Fico formed his first government, which brought together the populists of the ĽS-HZDS and the nationalists of the SNS (História vlád SR, 2024). The regional elections at the end of 2009 took place six months prior to the election of a new National Council in June 2010. As a result, the political competition for regional mandates and Župans in 2009 became, to some extent, a contest for electoral influence in the forthcoming parliamentary elections of 2010.

In the 2009 regional elections, there was a reduction in the number of deputies elected compared to the previous elections. A total of 408 deputies were elected to the Regional Assemblies. Notably, these changes impacted only two regions – Bratislava and Nitra. Specifically, in the Bratislava region, the number of deputies decreased by six, resulting in a total of 44. Conversely, in the Nitra region, two deputies were added to the Regional Assembly.

The recent regional elections saw the pro-government SMER-SD Party emerge as a key player in forming electoral coalitions. This party formed coalitions with other political entities, including populists ĽS-HZDS, occasional partners such as the nationalists SNS, and former partners of Vladimír Mečiar HZD. Opposition political forces traditionally aligned in centre-right coalitions, with participation from KDH and SDKÚ-DS. Additionally, the political representation of ethnic Hungarians expanded to include the newly formed liberal-conservative force, MOST-HÍD, advocating for dialogue and collaboration between Slovaks and Hungarians, alongside the traditional SMK-MKP (My sme MOST-HÍD, 2024). In the context of political narratives, MOST-HÍD advocates a more moderate ideology and appears less nationalistic than SMK-MKP. Furthermore, it is noteworthy that independent candidates experienced a surge in electoral support, ultimately securing 13.48% of all mandates. In specific regions, independent candidates displayed significant competitive prowess, garnering over 20% of the mandates in the Regional Assemblies of Trenčín and Košice.

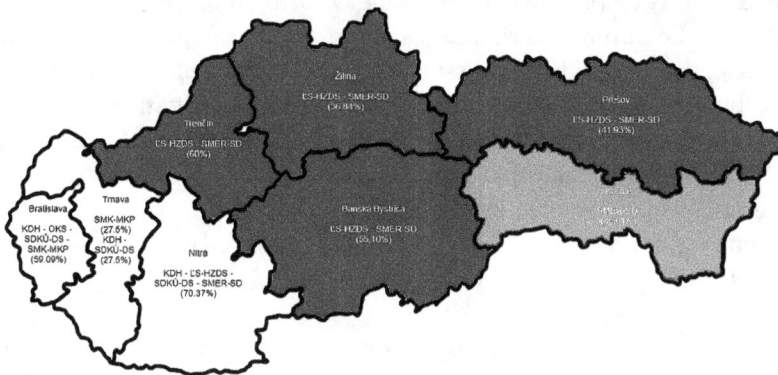

Figure 4. Electoral Map of the Slovak Regions According to the 2009 Regional Elections[19].

Source: the author's calculations are based on the Statistical Office of the Slovak Republic (Voľby a referendá).

---

19 The winners (independent candidates or political forces) in the regions are given. In each region, the electoral results indicate the percentage of mandates obtained by the political party or electoral coalition that secured the highest number of seats in the Regional Assembly. These figures represent the proportion of received mandates in relation to the entire composition of the Regional Assembly.

We are attempting to categorize the regions of the Slovak Republic into two groups based on the outcomes of the 2009 regional elections:

(1) Electorally homogeneous regions are regions with a noticeable advantage of one party. In 2009, the regions were divided into two equal groups, with Bratislava, Trenčín, Nitra, and Banská Bystrica being identified as electorally homogeneous. Nitra emerged as the most electorally homogeneous, characterized by a persistent electoral cleavage involving a multi-ideological electoral coalition pitted against the party representing the Hungarian ethnic minority. Notably, a four-party coalition comprising KDH, ĽS-HZDS, SDKÚ-DS, and SMER-SD confronted SMK-MKP. The multi-ideological coalition garnered support from two-thirds of the voters and secured 70.37% of all mandates. In the Trenčín region, Robert Fico's government partners, ĽS-HZDS and SMER-SD, collectively secured 60% of the seats in the Regional Assembly, while independent candidates won 10 seats, surpassing the opposition forces KDH and SDKÚ-DS, which secured 8 seats. Moving to the Bratislava region, the centre-right electoral union received nearly double the number of mandates compared to the pro-government conservatives, with 59% versus 31%. This pattern of liberal-conservative forces prevailing over populists and conservatives is a customary occurrence in the capital region. However, the Banská Bystrica region exhibited support for populists and conservatives, demonstrated by the electoral coalition ĽS-HZDS and SMER-SD securing the majority of mandates with 55.10%. Their closest competitors, SMK-MKP, only received 14.28% of the deputy seats in the Regional Assembly.

(2) In electorally heterogeneous regions, no single party or electoral bloc secures a majority of mandates in the Regional Assembly. The contest for mandates in the Regional Assembly of the Trnava region was highly competitive. Three political forces each secured a nearly equal number of parliamentary seats. Specifically, the party of ethnic Hungarians, SMK-MKP, and the centre-right coalition comprising KDH and SDKÚ-DS, both attained 11 mandates, constituting 27.50% of the seats. The broad conservative coalition, led by SMER-SD, secured one mandate less. In the Žilina region, the majority of mandates were divided between the two primary electoral coalitions. ĽS-HZDS and SMER-SD secured

36.84% of seats in the Regional Assembly (21 mandates), while the right-wing centrist coalition of KDH–OKS–SDKÚ-DS obtained 31.57% of seats (18 mandates). Independent deputies claimed the third position, acquiring 11 seats (19.29% of the seats) in the Žilina region. Notably, no clear leader emerged in the two Eastern Slovak regions with regards to winning the majority of mandates. In the Prešov region, the centre-right KDH–SDKÚ-DS received 40.32% of mandates, and the conservative and populist ĽS-HZDS garnered 41.93% of mandates. Furthermore, electoral deviations were observed in the Prešov region. For instance, the Roma minority party SRK, despite its substantial size and relatively low political participation in the region, managed to secure one mandate in the Regional Assembly (Strana rómskej koalície, 2024). Similarly, the local communist-radical party ÚSVIT also secured a mandate, with its office situated in Humenne, in the far eastern part of the country (Politická strana ÚSVIT, 2024). In the Košice region, the incumbent Prime Minister's party, SMER-SD, emerged as the clear winner. The Slovak social democrats secured 26 out of 57 possible mandates, representing 45.61% of the seats in the Regional Assembly. The decline in support for right-wing centrists or populist conservatives is evident from the fact that independent deputies claimed second place with 22.80% of the seats in the Regional Assembly.

Notably, during the 2009 regional elections, half the Župans were elected in the first round of voting (see Table 7). Candidates vying for the position of Župan were able to secure the support of over 50% of the electorate in the Trnava, Nitra, Žilina, and Košice regions.

In the Košice region, Zdenko Trebuľa was successfully re-elected as Župan, having attained the highest number of votes. The representative of SMER-SD garnered 60.25% of the votes. Similarly, in the Žilina region, SMER-SD's Juraj Blanár secured victory with 60.20% of the votes, commencing his second term as Župan. Milan Belica, also of SMER-SD, attained his third consecutive term as Župan in the Nitra region, receiving support from 60.27% of voters through a poly-ideological coalition of SMER-SD, SDKÚ-DS, and KDH. In the neighbouring Trnava region, independent candidate Tibor Mikuš secured his second term as Župan with just over 50% of the votes (52.99%).

Table 7. Župans Elected in the Regions of the Slovak Republic (according to the results of the 2009 regional elections).

Župan	Region	Voting Rounds	Party/Electoral Coalition	Votes (%)
Pavol Frešo	Bratislava	2	KDH–OKS–SaS–**SDKÚ-DS**–SMK-MKP[9]	60.50
Tibor Mikuš	Trnava	1	Independent	52.99
Pavol Sedláček	Trenčín	2	ANO–**ĽS-HZDS**–SNS–ZSNS	59.08
Milan Belica[10]	Nitra	1	**SMER**–SDKÚ-DS–KDH	60.27
Juraj Blanár	Žilina	1	**SMER**–SNS–ĽS-HZDS–HZDS–SZ–SF	63.20
Vladimír Maňka	Banská Bystrica	2	ĽS-HZDS–SMER	53.70
Peter Chudík	Prešov	2	HZD–ĽS-HZDS–**SMER**–SZS	54.06
Zdenko Trebuľa	Košice	1	**SMER**–SMK-MKP–ĽS-HZDS–SF–HZD–MOST-HÍD–LIGA	60.25

Source: the author's calculations are based on the Statistical Office of the Slovak Republic (Voľby a referendá).

The other four regions held a second round of voting to determine the winner on 28 November, with an 18.29% voter turnout. It is worth noting that during the second round, the competition for the position of Župan occurred only in the Prešov and Banská Bystrica regions. In the Eastern Slovak region, Peter Chudík, backed by the conservative coalition led by SMER-SD, achieved his third consecutive triumph with 54.06% of the vote, while his closest rival, Ján Hudacký from the centre-right coalition, secured 45.93% of the support. In the capital Bratislava region, SDKÚ-DS representative Pavol Frešo was elected Župan for the first time, garnering 60.50% of the support. It is noteworthy that he was a seasoned politician first elected to the parliament of the Slovak Republic in 2006 (Frešo, 2024). The incumbent Župan, Vladimír Bajan, lost to Pavol Frešo by more than 20% of the votes (39.49%). In the northern Trenčín region, Pavol Sedláček from the populist-conservative

20 The newly elected Župan is a member of the party highlighted in bold.
21 Župans who have been elected for the second or third consecutive term are highlighted in italics.

electoral alliance ĽS-HZDS–SMER-SD was re-elected with 59.08%. In the Banská Bystrica region, Vladimír Maňka (53.70%) from SMER-SD was elected Župan. He was a well-known Slovak politician closely related to social democracy. He was elected both to the parliament of the Slovak Republic and the European Parliament (Maňka, 2024). His closest rival, right-centrist Jozef Mikuš, was over 7% behind him (46.29%).

2.4 2013 Elections

The regional elections in 2013 were conducted just like previous ones, taking place before the Christmas and New Year celebrations. All regions held two rounds of voting. The first round occurred on 9 November, with the second round taking place in some regions on 23 November, 2013. The voter turnout for the first round was 20.11%, and for the second round, it was slightly lower at 17.29% (2013 – Voľby do orgánov). In general, in terms of organizing the electoral process, the 2013 regional elections met the standards set by the 2009 elections.

In the lead-up to the 2013 regional elections, the political landscape in the Slovak Republic was characterized by the dominance of the SMER-SD Party. Following the results of the 2012 early elections to the National Council, the Slovak Social Democrats established a single-party government under the leadership of Robert Fico[22] (2012 – Voľby do NR SR). This marked the second premiership for Fico. In the 2010s, the ideological convergence of right-wing and left-wing parties in the Slovak Republic set the stage for the potential radicalization of the party landscape (Martinkovič, 2021, p. 68). Political parties with well-defined ideologies, such as the social-democratic SMER-SD, were transforming "catch-all parties" and populist political forces. However, Robert Fico's reputation became slightly controversial due to his involvement in various scandals, including the "Gorilla scandal" in 2011 (Slovak politics...,

---

22 44.41% voters supported SMER–SD.

2012). Nevertheless, these issues did not diminish his significant influence in Slovak politics and government. It was against this backdrop that regular elections for the Regional Assemblies were conducted.

The number of deputies in the Regional Assemblies elected in the 2013 regional elections did not change. Similar to the previous elections in 2009, a total of 408 deputies were elected, with the highest number of 62 deputies in the Prešov region and the lowest number of 40 deputies in the Trnava region.

On the eve of the regional elections, the electoral strategies of certain parties underwent some changes. For instance, due to the strong influence of SMER-SD in parliament and government, the party focused on promoting its party list. Unlike previous elections, SMER-SD ran independently in six out of eight regions. However, participating in electoral coalitions also proved to be fruitful for SMER-SD. This was evident in the formation of a two-party coalition, SMER-SD–KDH, comprised of ideologically diverse parties in the Nitra and Banská Bystrica regions. This election strategy was

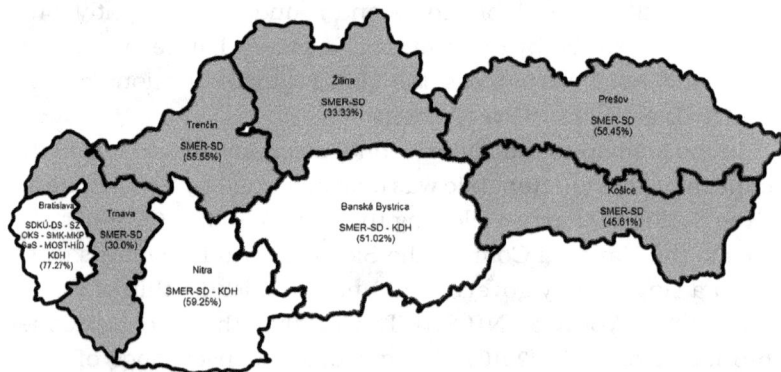

Figure 5. Electoral Map of the Slovak Regions According to the 2013 Regional Elections.[23]

Source: the author's calculations are based on the Statistical Office of the Slovak Republic (Voľby a referendá).

---

23 The winners (independent candidates or political forces) in the regions are given. Marking of the regions: in each region, the electoral results indicate the percentage of mandates obtained by the political party or electoral coalition that secured the highest number of seats in the Regional Assembly. These figures represent the proportion of received mandates in relation to the entire composition of the Regional Assembly.

successful, as the coalition garnered the majority of votes (more than 50%) in both regions. Conversely, the opposition party, SD-KÚ-DS, sought centre-right allies. The christian democrats KDH, along with the liberal-conservatives from the Hungarian minority party MOST-HÍD, largely joined forces with them. Apart from the traditional political contests, it was expected that the number of independent deputies would increase based on the trends observed in previous regional elections.

Based on the outcomes of the 2013 regional elections, it is evident that the regions of the Slovak Republic can be categorized into two distinct groups:

(1) In the 2013 election, there were regions where one political party dominated and received 50% or more of the mandates. In five out of eight regions, a single political party obtained the majority of seats in the Regional Assembly. The clearest example of this was in the Bratislava region, where a broad centre-right coalition made up of seven parties won 34 out of 44 possible seats (77.27%) in the Regional Assembly[24]. The main aim of uniting all right-centrist parties was to challenge the dominance of SMER-SD in the country. This strategy proved effective, as the social democrats only managed to secure one mandate. In four other regions, SMER-SD or coalitions involving SMER-SD obtained the majority of mandates in the Regional Assembly. In the Trenčín region, SMER-SD independently secured 25 out of 45 mandates, which accounted for 55.55% of the seats. The right-centrist parties significantly lagged behind the Social Democrats with only eight mandates, while independent deputies came in second place with 11 mandates. In the Prešov region, SMER-SD won all 35 mandates out of 62 possible, which is 56.45% of parliamentary seats. However, in this Eastern Slovak region, the Christian-democratic ideology has always been electorally stable. As a result, the electoral coalition consisting of KDH was able to secure 19 mandates. In the Nitra and Banská Bystrica regions, the two-party coalition SMER-SD–KDH emerged as the winner. The coalition received 32 mandates out of 54 possible, which accounted for 59.25% of parliamentary seats. In the case of the Western Slovakian region, the two highest-ranking parties joined forces to combat the most influential party of the Hungar-

24 Coalition: SDKÚ-DS–SZ–OKS–SMK-MKP–SaS–MOST-HÍD–KDH.

ian minority, SMK-MKP. Such multi-ideological electoral alliances are often formed in the Nitrian region. Meanwhile, the Banská Bystrica region was an electoral union of the highest-rated parties that secured a majority in the Regional Assembly. The coalition was able to obtain 25 deputy mandates out of 49, whereas independent deputies secured 13 mandates, placing them second.

(2) Electorally heterogeneous regions. In the 2013 regional elections, only three regions were characterized as electorally heterogeneous, indicating that no single political force secured a majority in their respective Regional Assemblies. Among these regions, the Žilina region stood out for its particularly scattered vote, with five political forces and a group of independent deputies all obtaining mandates. The victorious party was SMER-SD, which garnered a third of the seats in the Regional Assembly (19 out of 57 mandates). Notably, independent deputies in the Žilina region achieved the country's best result, securing 28.07% of the deputies' seats. A significant political competition unfolded in the Košice region of Eastern Slovakia. Four political parties and a group of independent candidates successfully secured mandates. SMER-SD emerged as the clear winner, narrowly missing out on a majority in the Regional Assembly with 26 mandates out of 57 possible (constituting 45.51% of the vote). Meanwhile, in the Trnava region, there was a close race between SMER-SD, which secured 12 mandates out of 40 (30% of the Regional Assembly), and the SMK-MKP party representing the Hungarian minority, which secured 11 mandates (27.50%). Additionally, the liberal-conservative Hungarian party MOST-HÍD secured four seats, constituting 10% of the Regional Assembly.

The 2013 regional elections underscored the growing influence of independent deputies and signalled their prospective significance in future electoral processes. Independent candidates secured 17.89% of all mandates in the Regional Assembly. Notably, independent candidates in Bratislava, Trenčín, Žilina, and Banská Bystrica achieved the second-highest number of mandates. This outcome signifies the positive trend of increasing electoral trust in independent candidates during each successive regional election.

In the 2013 Župan elections, the results were similar to the 2009 regional elections. Three out of eight Župans were elected in the first round of voting. In the Trenčín, Žilina, and Prešov regions, the majority of voters supported the candidates for the Župan position (see Table 8).

Table 8. Župans Elected in the Regions of the Slovak Republic (according to the results of the 2013 regional elections).

Župan	Region	Voting Round	Party/Electoral Coalition	Votes (%)
Pavol Frešo[25]	Bratislava	2	KDH–SZ–SMK-MKP-**SDKÚ-DS**–SaS–OKS–MOST-HÍD[26]	74.24
Tibor Mikuš	Trnava	2	Independent	60.26
Jaroslav Baška	Trenčín	1	**SMER-SD**	53.45
Milan Belica	Nitra	2	**SMER-SD**	55.61
Juraj Blanár	Žilina	1	**SMER-SD–SZ–SNS**	54.01
Marian Kotleba	Banská Bystrica	2	**ĽSNS**	55.53
Peter Chudík	Prešov	1	**SMER-SD**–SMS–NÁŠ KRAJ	53.78
Zdenko Trebuľa	Košice	2	MOST- HÍD–SMK-MKP–**SMER-SD**	53.07

Source: the author's calculations are based on the Statistical Office of the Slovak Republic (Voľby a referendá).

In the first round, it is noteworthy that each of the elected Župans only slightly surpassed the 50% threshold. Jaroslav Baška from SMER-SD secured his first term as Župan in the Trenčín region. His political career has been closely aligned with SMER-SD at both the local and national levels. J. Baška was elected to the National Council representing the Slovak Social Democrats and, from 2008 to 2010, held the position of Minister of Defence of the Slovak Republic (Baška, 2024). Since 2013, Baška has increasingly focused on regional politics and was elected Župan in the Trenčín region for the first time. In the Prešov region, Peter Chudík, representing SMER-SD, secured his fourth consecutive term as Župan, establishing an electoral record at the regional level. P. Chudík faced minimal competition from the Christian Democrat candi-

---

25 Župans elected for the second, third, or fourth consecutive term are highlighted in italics.
26 The newly elected Župan is a member of the party highlighted in bold.

date, Ján Hudacký, who garnered just over 30% of the votes, resulting in Chudík's victory in the first round. In the Žilina region,
Juraj Blanár, also representing SMER-SD, secured his third consecutive term as Župan, defeating his closest competitor, Miroslav
Mikolášik from KDH, by a significant margin of 54% to 24%.

In five other regions, a second round of voting was necessary
to elect a Župan. Notably, Pavol Frešo received overwhelming
electoral support in the Bratislava region, securing a second consecutive term with 74.24% of the votes. His opponent was the female politician Monika Flašíková-Beňová from SMER-SD, which
is unusual for Slovak politics when it comes to the post of Župan.
The choice of a woman may have been intentional, considering the
"progressiveness" of the capital region. However, this approach
did not bring SMER-SD success in the capital region, especially
since there were only two female candidates in the first round of
voting. In the Trnava region, Tibor Mikuš secured nearly twice
the electoral support, garnering 60.26% of the vote, marking his
third consecutive term as Župan. In the 2009 elections, he ran as
an independent candidate. The second round of elections in the
remaining three regions saw marginal differences in support for
the candidates, ranging from 7% to 9%. Milan Belica of SMER-SD
was re-elected for the fourth time in the Nitra region with 55.61% of
the vote. Tomáš Galbavý, representing SDKÚ-DS, his competitor,
managed to secure the support of the Hungarian ethnic minority.
Similarly, Nitra voters reaffirmed Milan Belica's position for the
fourth consecutive term. In the Košice region, Zdenko Trebuľa was
re-elected as Župan for the third term in a row, securing 53.07%
of the vote. Rudolf Bauer, nominated by the Slovak conservative
KDS, posed substantial competition, receiving 46.92% of the vote
and challenging the incumbent Župan of Košice.

The most surprising result was the election of Marian Kotleba as the Župan in the Banská Bystrica region. He managed to
defeat the previous Župan, Vladimír Maňka, with 55.53% of the
votes in the second round. This was quite unexpected as in the first
round, V. Maňka was only 0.53% short of winning, while Kotleba
had received only 21.30% at that time. Kotleba has emerged as
a prominent figure in Slovak politics, representing radical right-
wing ideologies and anti-Western sentiments. His election to the
Slovak parliament through the ĽSNS and Kotlebovci projects un-

derscores his influence in filling an electoral radical right-wing void within the country's political landscape (Kotleba, 2024). The proliferation of right-wing radical ideologies within Slovak society is frequently attributed to a widespread crisis in the public understanding of democratic principles (Jahelka, 2021, p. 162). In the 2013 regional elections, the right-wing populist Marian Kotleba secured the highest administrative position in one of Slovakia's largest regions. Concurrently, voters in Banská Bystrica elected a "native" politician to represent their interests.

2.5 2017 Elections

The penultimate regional elections took place on 4 November, 2017, and became symbolic for the Slovak Republic in many respects. Firstly, they marked the highest voter turnout (29.95%) since the first regional elections in 2001 (2017 – Voľby do orgánov). In the regional elections, one out of every three voters participated, a figure deemed modest for national elections but indicative of a positive trend for regional elections. The low voter turnout prompts the need for discussions on the viability of direct regional elections versus indirect ones (Cirner & Dudinská, 2018, p. 50). The 2017 regional elections witnessed substantial regulatory modifications initiated by the government of Robert Fico, involving deputies from SMER-SD and MOST-HÍD in 2016. These changes entailed a reduction in the frequency of voting, with regional elections now being executed in a single round of voting. Consequently, the candidate securing the highest number of votes was elected as Župan. The primary rationale behind these regulatory adjustments was the government's aspiration to economize on regional elections. To illustrate, they referenced data from the previous regional elections in 2013, highlighting a potential cost saving of 2.4 billion Euros had the second round of voting been omitted (Kto komu pomôže..., 2016). The introduction of the option to elect Župans was aimed at encouraging voter participation in the elections with promptness. Historically, the turnout for the second round of regional elections has been relatively low, typically ranging from 10% to 15%. Moreover, the shift to single-round voting may potentially bolster the position of SMER-SD, as five Župans affiliated with this party have held office since 2013. In addition, single-round voting has had an impact on the legitimacy of the Župans elected in 2017.

The political landscape preceding the 2017 regional elections reaffirmed the continued influence of Robert Fico and his party, SMER-SD. Following the parliamentary elections of 2016, SMER-SD secured victory once more, albeit with a reduced level of support at 28.28% (2016 – Voľby do NR SR). Subsequently, the third government, under the leadership of Robert Fico, was established, allowing SMER-SD to retain its influence on the political landscape in the Slovak Republic. However, Robert Fico's third term was characterized by ambiguity and government scandals, particularly the incident in the summer of 2017 involving the allocation of European funds by the Ministry of Education and Science (Kapitán, 2017). Prior to the 2017 regional elections, a corruption scandal related to the government of Robert Fico had already damaged the trust of Slovak voters in the SMER-SD candidates. Following the regional elections, the Slovak Republic was rocked by a highly sensitive scandal involving the murder of investigative journalist Ján Kuciak in February 2018. This scandal ultimately led to the resignation of Prime Minister R. Fico and triggered a protracted political crisis in the Slovak Republic.

In the 2017 regional elections, a record 416 deputies were elected to Regional Assemblies, signifying the highest number of mandates in the history of regional elections. When compared to the 2013 elections, the number of mandates in the Bratislava region increased by six, and by two in the Trenčín region. Notably, there were no quantitative changes in the composition of Regional Assemblies in the remaining six regions.

The 2017 regional elections revealed new electoral trends in the formulation of electoral strategies by political parties/blocs and independent candidates. It is evident that the elections occurred against a backdrop of declining confidence among Slovak voters in political parties. Notably, independent candidates emerged as the clear victors for the first time in the history of regional elections, doing so by a significant margin. While previous election campaigns saw independent candidates garnering limited electoral support, the 2017 elections positioned them as frontrunners.

The 2017 regional elections confirmed the crisis of political parties' ideologies and the search for "independent faces" in Slovak
regional politics (Martinkovič, 2018, p. 40). Additionally, the SMER-
SD government secured votes by effectively fielding independent
candidates in the Žilina, Banská Bystrica, Trenčín, and Prešov regions. In the Trenčín and Nitra regions, SMER-SD is a prominent
political force that forges electoral alliances with the nationalist
SNS and the liberal-conservative Hungarians MOST-HÍD, mirror-
ing the coalition format of the third government of Robert Fico.
SMER-SD was unsuccessful only in the Bratislava and Nitra regions. The christian democrats KDH, the liberal-conservative SaS,
and the burgeoning populists OĽaNO have emerged as the primary electoral alternative to the Slovak social democrats. This triumvirate frequently forms electoral coalitions, sometimes incorporating less influential political entities.

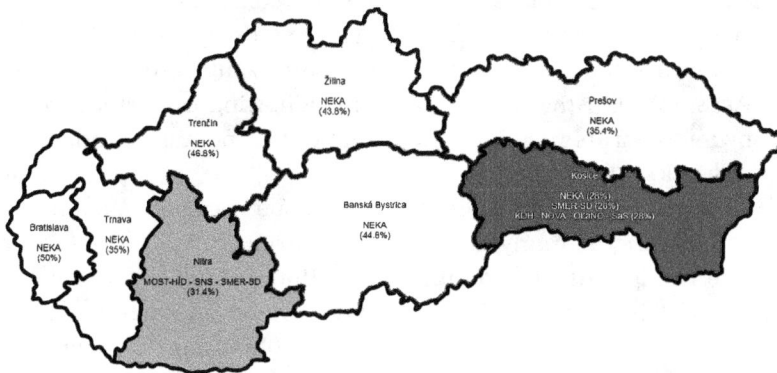

Figure 6. Electoral Map of the Slovak Regions According to the 2017 Regional
Elections[27].

Source: the author's calculations are based on the Statistical Office of the Slovak Republic (Voľby
a referendá).

In the past, we have attempted to categorize the regions of the
Slovak Republic based on the results of regional elections into

27 The winners (independent candidates or political forces) in the regions are
given. Marking of the regions: In each region, the electoral results indicate the
percentage of mandates obtained by the political party or electoral coalition
that secured the highest number of seats in the Regional Assembly. These
figures represent the proportion of received mandates in relation to the entire
composition of the Regional Assembly.

either electorally homogeneous or electorally heterogeneous regions. However, the 2017 elections revealed a dominant pattern of electoral heterogeneity in most regions. In seven out of eight regions, no political force, electoral block, or group of independent deputies managed to secure half (or slightly more) of the voters' votes. Only the capital Bratislava region can be considered an electorally homogeneous region, and even this classification is based on minimal indicators (50% of votes).

In the Bratislava region, independent candidates attained 25 out of 50 available mandates, representing the highest tally of independent deputies in the Regional Assemblies. Historically, in the Bratislava region, the opposition garnered greater electoral support than pro-government forces. The electoral coalition comprising KDH, OĽaNO, and SaS secured 17 mandates, while the electoral coalition aligned with SMER-SD only obtained six mandates in the Regional Assembly. These outcomes affirm a "protest vote" against conservative pro-government forces and underscore a preference for appointing non-partisan deputies to the Regional Assembly. On the other hand, the right-wing opposition coalition demonstrates evident Eurosceptic and populist tendencies (Marušiak, 2018, p. 25).

The group of electorally heterogeneous regions is extensive, encompassing as many as seven regions. Our analysis will focus on the voting patterns spanning from the western to the eastern regions of the country. In the Trnava region, independent candidates secured victory in most regions, obtaining 14 mandates, which accounts for 35% of the parliamentary seats. The competing parties and coalitions experienced minimal success. The SMK-MKP, backed by the strong political influence of the Hungarian minority, attained the second position with 13 seats, while the opposition electoral coalition[28] secured third place with 11 seats.

Notably, SMER-SD faced an electoral setback in the Trnava region, only securing one mandate. The Nitra region emerged as the only region where an electoral coalition, rather than independent deputies, emerged as the sole winner. This outcome is consistent with previous election campaigns, reflecting the significant political influence of the Hungarian ethnic minority. In the region, the

---

28 Coalition: KDH–OKS–OĽaNO–SaS–Zmena zdola–DÚ

pro-government coalition, including the "moderate Hungarians" MOST-HÍD (17 mandates/31.48% of parliamentary seats), prevails. The more conservative SMK-MKP has secured 11 seats, while the opposition forces[29] have obtained one less. In the Nitra region, the "Hungarian factor" and the prevailing all-Slovak electoral trend of independent candidates have become intricately intertwined. Consequently, the votes have been dispersed among four distinct political forces.

In the Trenčín and Žilina regions, conservative political forces, such as Mečiar's ĽS-HZDS and the party of "social populists" SMER-SD, received significant support from the majority of the electorate. Notably, independent candidates garnered the primary electoral support, securing 22 mandates (55% of parliamentary seats) in the Trenčín region and 25 mandates (43.85% of parliamentary seats) in the Žilina region. In the Trenčín region, only two electoral coalitions succeeded in obtaining mandates, with the pro-government coalition, with SMER-SD, securing 16 mandates[30], while the opposition coalition[31] managed to secure nine mandates. In the Žilina region, the SMER-SD Party ran independently and secured ten mandates. The nationalist SNS Party also obtained five mandates. The opposition coalition secured 17 mandates, coming second after the independent candidates. Consequently, both regions, known for their conservative stances, ultimately lent their support to independent candidates.

The central Slovak Banská Bystrica region presented a notably diverse landscape in its recent voting process. Notably, in addition to independent candidates, six distinct political forces were successful in securing representation in the Regional Assembly. Among these, only SMER-SD, with 15 mandates accounting for 30.61% of deputy seats, emerged as a significant contender to independent candidates. The opposition coalition[32] yielded to the Hungarian ethnic minority party SMK-MKP, which secured five seats, while the coalition itself won four. Furthermore, the right-wing radical ĽSNS and the traditional Slovak nationalists SNS

---

29 Coalition: KDH–NOVA–OKS–OĽaNO–SaS–ŠANCA
30 Coalition: MOST-HÍD–SNS–SMER-SD–SZ
31 Coalition: KDH–NOVA–OKS–OĽaNO–SaS–Zmena zdola–DÚ
32 Coalition: KDH–NOVA–OKS–OĽaNO–SaS

both obtained one mandate each, with the liberal-conservative MOST-HÍD also securing a single mandate.

In the 2017 election, the eastern region of the country maintained its historical electoral preferences while also showing increased support for independent candidates. Independent candidates and nominees from established political entities were nearly neck and neck in electoral representation. Notably, in the Košice region, a triumvirate occurred, with equal support garnered by independent candidates, SMER-SD, and the opposition coalition[33], resulting in each securing 16 mandates, accounting for 28% of the seats in Regional Assemblies. The liberal-conservative Hungarian party MOST-HÍD attempted to introduce some competition for the three dominant political forces in Slovakia. They achieved their best result by securing six seats while running independently. This was their strongest showing across the entire country. In the neighbouring Prešov region, independent candidates narrowly outperformed the opposition coalition[34], winning by just one seat. Independents secured 22 mandates out of 35.48 parliamentary seats, while the opposition coalition received 21 mandates. SMER-SD experienced a decrease in support, obtaining only 16 mandates. Additionally, the right-wing nationalist party SNS secured two mandates, and the radical leftist party ÚSVIT won one mandate. Independent deputies held prominent positions across the country, including in the eastern regions. However, the difference in votes between independent candidates and traditional political parties/coalitions was not notably significant.

In the 2017 regional elections, it is worth noting that Župans were elected based on the results of a single round according to the principle of relative majority of votes received. It is essential to investigate whether the alteration in the election method had a substantive impact on the elected Župans (see Table 9).

The modification in the format of the Župan elections, entailing the shift to a single round of voting, had a profound impact on the election outcome. None of the candidates managed to secure an outright majority of votes, as no candidate succeeded in garnering 50% of the voter support. Consequently, none of them would have

---

33 Coalition: KDH–NOVA–OĽaNO–SaS
34 Coalition: KDH–NOVA–OĽaNO–SaS

Table 9. Župans Elected in the Regions of the Slovak Republic (according to the results of the 2017 regional elections).

Župan	Region	Voting Round	Party/Electoral Coalition	Votes (%)
Juraj Droba	Bratisla-va	–	**SaS**-OĽaNO-SMK-MKP-NOVA-OKS-Zmena zdola-DÚ[35]	20.42
Jozef Viskupič	Trnava	–	**OĽaNO**-SaS-KDH-OKS-Zmena zdola-DÚ	42.90
Jaroslav Baška[36]	Trenčín	–	**SMER-SD**-SNS-MOST-HÍD-SZ	49.98
Milan Belica	Nitra	–	**SMER-SD**-SNS-MOST-HÍD	34.10
Erika Jurinová	Žilina	–	**OĽaNO**-SaS-KDH-OKS, NOVA	43.67
Ján Lunter	Banská Bystrica	–	Independent	48.53
Milan Majerský	Prešov	–	**KDH**-SaS-OĽaNO-NOVA	40.36
Rastislav Trnka	Košice	–	**Independent** / OĽaNO-SaS-KDH-NOVA-ŠANCA	37.80

Source: the author's calculations are based on the Statistical Office of the Slovak Republic (Voľby a referendá).

been elected under the conditions of a two-round voting system. Jaroslav Baška, the incumbent Župan in the Trenčín region, came closest to achieving 50% of the votes, falling short by only 0.02%. Similarly, Ján Lunter, the newly elected Župan of the Banská Bystrica region, was close to the 50% mark, with a deficit of just 1.47%. Juraj Droba, elected as the Župan in the Bratislava region, exhibited the least legitimacy as he was supported by only a fifth of the voters in the capital region. [35] [36]

In the 2017 elections, the "unlimited" tenure of a Župan effectively ended as elections were held in one round only. The results showed that Župans were elected for the next term only in the Trenčín region (Jaroslav Baška) and Nitra region (Milan Belica). New Župans were elected in the Bratislava, Trnava, Žilina, Banská

---

35 The newly elected Župan is a member of the party highlighted in bold.
36 Župans who were elected for multiple consecutive terms are highlighted in italics.

Bystrica, and Prešov regions, as the incumbent Župans in those areas ran for re-election but were not successful. Only in the Košice region did the current Župan, Zdenko Trebuľa, not participate in the elections. These electoral statistics suggest that strong and influential candidates are focusing on the second round of voting. Before the 2017 regional elections, the primary goal for influential candidates, especially incumbent Župans, was to advance to the second round of voting.

In the Bratislava region, an intriguing scenario unfolded with the election of Župans. The votes were divided among five candidates, with the lowest receiving 15.97% and the winner achieving 20.42% of the vote. Juraj Droba ran as part of a united coalition with SaS and OĽaNO. Notably, among the top five candidates, only independent candidates opposed the newly elected Župan. Juraj Droba is a well-known Slovak politician and a co-founder of the liberal-conservative SaS. He previously served as a member of the National Council of the Slovak Republic from SaS (Droba, 2024). In general, Droba's political image is consistent with the prevalent liberal inclinations of voters in the Slovak capital.

In 2017, there was a change in leadership in the Trnava region as Tibor Mikuš, an independent, concluded his long-term tenure as Župan. The successful candidate in the election was Jozef Viskupič, a member of OĽaNO at the time, who was gradually gaining political influence. Prior to assuming his role as a regional politician, J. Viskupič served as a deputy in the National Council for multiple terms. Notably, during the early 2010s, he was among the influential politicians who left the SaS Party to join Igor Matovič's OĽaNO political initiative (Matovič, 2024). In 2017, Jozef Viskupič achieved one of the highest vote shares in the country, surpassing 40%.

Milan Belica was re-elected as the Župan of the Nitra region, making it one of only two Slovak regions where the incumbent Župan was re-elected for a new term. He had been in office since the first elections in 2001 and won four consecutive terms. He started his fifth term in 2017 with 34.10% of the vote, representing the SMER-SD Party. Despite not receiving significant support, he still outperformed his main rival, Ján Grešo, from the centre-right coalition of SaS, OĽaNO, and KDH, who garnered around 17% of the votes.

In the Trenčín region, Jaroslav Baška from SMER-SD was re-elected as Župan for a second term, having secured just under 50% of the votes (49.98%). Renáta Kaščáková, the candidate from the centre-right coalition, received 25.13% of the votes. In the Žilina region, Erika Jurinová, supported by OĽaNO–SaS–KDH, made history by becoming the first female Župan with the support of 43.67% of voters. Notably, Erika Jurinová has served in the National Council since 2010, initially representing SaS and later OĽaNO (Jurinová, 2024). Only 29.77% of the voters supported the incumbent Župan Juraj Blanár from SMER-SD.

An interesting struggle for the position of Župan has unfolded in the Banská Bystrica region. The incumbent Župan, Marian Kotleba, is a well-known right-wing radical politician in the Slovak Republic, and this was reflected even during his term in office. Kotleba was accused of exceeding his powers and putting pressure on freedom of speech. He was in constant conflict with the regional theatre community and the Ministry of Culture (Rehák, 2015). Kotleba faced frequent accusations of ideological commitment, particularly pertaining to his alleged anti-Roma sentiments and anti-Americanism. These allegations were seen as contradictory to his role as Župan (Vražda, 2015). Prior to the 2017 elections, three prominent independent candidates, Ján Lunter, Martin Klus, and Stanislav Mičev, made a collective decision to unite in opposition to Marian Kotleba by nominating the most influential candidate among them (Pataj, 2017). The election results show that Ján Lunter won with 48.53% of the votes, becoming the new Župan. Kotleba received 23.24% of the votes. Lunter emphasized the need to address the critical socio-economic issues in the Banská Bystrica region immediately after the election.

In the eastern region of the Slovak Republic, specifically in the Prešov region, Peter Chudík's many years' tenure as Župan has come to an end. The SMER-SD representative held the position of Župan for a total of 16 years, having been initially elected in 2001. Milan Majerský, a representative of the christian democrats of KDH, emerged victorious, effectively unseating the long-serving Župan. Christian democracy has historically enjoyed popularity in this eastern Slovak region, providing a substantive alternative to SMER-SD. Majerský attained 40.36% of the votes, while Chudík garnered 30.62%. Notably, Majerský's political trajectory is closely associated with KDH, where he assumed leadership in 2020 before being elected as a deputy to the National Council (KDH, 2024). However, following the early elections in 2023, he made the decision to shift his focus to regional politics.

In the Košice region of eastern Slovakia, there was a heated competition for the position of Župan. The main contenders were Richard Raši and Rastislav Trnka. Richard Raši is a close political ally of Robert Fico. He held ministerial positions in Fico's governments at various times and was elected to parliament from SMER-SD. In local politics, he is best known as the mayor of Košice (Košice, 2024). The young and promising independent candidate Rastislav Trnka ran against the experienced politician Richard Raši. R. Trnka's political experience was primarily focused on municipal politics in Košice. Ultimately, Rastislav Trnka secured victory over Richard Raši by a narrow margin of 875 votes, with the winner receiving 37.80% and the runner-up receiving 37.24%. R. Trnka was just 33 years old when he was elected as the Župan of one of the largest regions of the Slovak Republic.

3 Current Regional Elections of 2022 in the Slovak Republic

3.1 Political Fragmentation of Slovak Regions According to the 2022 Election Outcome

The results of the regional elections have demonstrated a significant level of distrust among Slovak voters towards traditional political parties. Many citizens are searching for "new faces" in the political arena. The deep political crisis of 2018, which was linked to the murder of investigative journalist Ján Kuciak and his partner, had a significant impact on the level of trust that Slovaks have in traditional politicians. The subsequent resignation of Robert Fico, along with the election of non-conventional politician Zuzana Čaputová as President, was expected to lead to a reform of the political system. However, the entry of Igor Matovič into parliament on a populist wave in 2020, with his party OĽaNO, only served to deepen the delegitimization of Slovak politicians. With the regional elections of 2022 approaching, voters would search for viable electoral alternatives. At the regional level of politics, individuals tended to focus on candidates who possessed a proven track record of effectively addressing the challenges that affect the region. In many regions, voters were inclined to elect politicians who had already served at least one term in the highest positions, such as Župans. Consequently, the level of support for national political parties was progressively declining.

The 2022 regional elections highlighted several issues concerning regional politics in the Slovak Republic and the Central European region. It is essential to enhance the authority of regional governments by clarifying their powers, improving their communication with the media, and finding better ways to engage with the public (Janas & Jánošková, 2024, p. 51). The outcome of the 2022 regional elections reaffirmed the tendency of Slovak voters to cast their votes in a personalized manner, largely influenced by the national political landscape. Notably, the parliamentary or non-parliamentary status of a political entity substantially influences voters' behaviour (Voitovych, 2023, p. 62).

The 2022 regional elections resulted in a clear win for independent deputies. They secured 159 mandates in the Regional Assemblies, which accounted for 37.94% of all deputy seats. The ethnic

Hungarian party, SZÖVETSÉG–ALIANCIA, secured the second position with 54 deputy mandates, 12.88% of the total representation in the Assemblies (Voľby a referendá). The electoral outcome presents a complex scenario where independent candidates managed to secure a first-place victory in only four regions. Additionally, in two other regions, they obtained an equal number of deputy mandates to their closest competitors (see Figure 7).

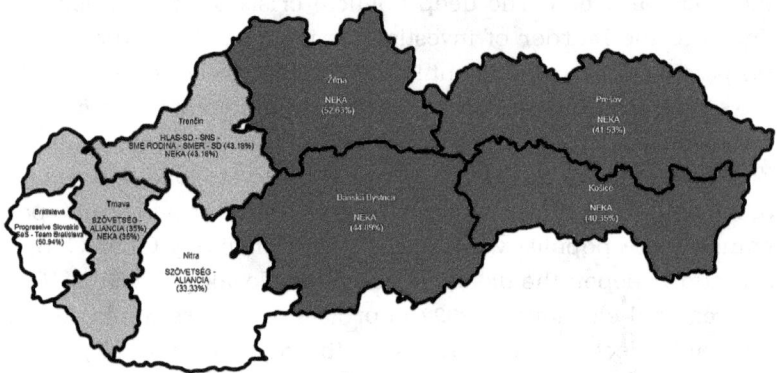

Figure 7. Electoral Map of the Slovak Regions According to the 2022 Regional Elections[37].

Source: the author's calculations are based on the Statistical Office of the Slovak Republic (Voľby a referendá).

It is notable that the eastern and central parts of the nation, which tend to support conservative or populist political forces, have shown their support for independent candidates. In this context, it is worth mentioning the unequivocal winners of the 2020 parliamentary elections in the Trenčín, Banská Bystrica, Prešov, and Košice regions – the populists OĽaNO, led by the controversial figure Igor Matovič, and the social populists SMER-SD, led by Robert Fico (Voľby a referendá). In the regional elections of 2022, independent candidates emerged as winners in the central and eastern regions of the country. This outcome can be interpreted as a reflection of the conservative or populist attitudes of local voters, as well as a loss of confidence in traditional political parties. In contrast, the Regional Assemblies elections saw a higher

---

37 The winners (independent candidates or political forces) in the regions are given.

level of trust in political parties, particularly in the Bratislava and Nitra regions. Notably, a three-member liberal-conservative coalition comprising Progresívne Slovensko, SaS, and the local TEAM Bratislava movement secured victory in the Bratislava region. In the region of Nitra, the political party SZÖVETSÉG–ALIANCIA, which represents the Hungarian minority, has emerged victorious in the 2022 elections. This outcome was expected, as the region is home to a significant population of Hungarians. SZÖVETSÉG–ALIANCIA is a political group that recently rebranded itself to represent a broad spectrum of Hungarian political interests. Interestingly, this win comes after the party failed to secure any seats in the National Council elections of 2020. As for two other regions in the western part of the Slovak Republic, no clear winner has emerged. In the Trnava region, however, independent candidates and members of SZÖVETSÉG–ALIANCIA have secured 14 mandates in the Regional Assembly. This is particularly noteworthy since a significant population of the Hungarian ethnic minority is located in the southern part of this region. In the Trenčín region, the distribution of mandates was equally divided (19 seats each) between independent candidates and a coalition comprising SNS nationalists, right-wing conservatives from Boris Kollár's SME RODINA, and nominal social democrats SMER-SD, HLAS-SD (see Figure 7).

The Župans were elected at the same time as the Regional Assemblies. In only three regions, the winners managed to obtain an absolute majority of the votes. In the Bratislava region, Juraj Droba from SaS and Progresívne Slovensko won with 63.6% of the votes, and he is now serving his second term. SMER-SD representative Jaroslav Baška has held the position of Župan in the Trenčín region since 2013, and this time he received the support of 67.25% of the voters. In the Košice region, Rastislav Trnka, who was elected by the Christian Democrats and the Hungarian minority party, celebrated his victory with 51.31% of the votes, and is serving for his second term. Ondrej Lunter, an independent candidate, was close to obtaining the support of half of the voters in the Banská Bystrica region, with 47.53% of the votes. It is worth noting the political background of some elected officials. For example, Ondrej succeeded his father, Ján Lunter, as Župan. In the Prešov region, Milan Majerský, representing the Christian Democrats KDH and the liberal-conservatives SME RODINA, received over 40% of the votes (42.01%) and was elected Župan for the second time. However, in other regions, the candidates for Župan did not receive significant electoral support. In the Trnava region, Jozef Viskupič from OĽANO was re-elected for a second term with a result of 38.56%. Meanwhile, Erika Jurinová from OĽaNO, the only female Župan, won just over 30% of the vote in the Žilina region and was re-elected as well. Branislav Becík, who ran for SMER-SD, received the least number of votes, with only 27.49% of voters supporting him. However, this was still enough for him to be elected as Župan.

3.2 Political Cleavage "Slovak Politics vs Hungarian Minority"

The Hungarian ethnic minority and the Slovak central government had always had longstanding but strained relations. In the post-socialist period, they developed into a long-lasting sociopolitical cleavage, dependent on Budapest rather than Bratislava and characterized by high political tension. With the return of the "old-new" Viktor Orbán to power in 2010, Slovakia embarked on an ambiguous strategy of supporting Hungarians in Slovakia, which, during this period, exacerbated tensions in Slovak–Hungarian relations.

Orbán's Hungary purposefully pursued a strategy of winning the sympathies of foreign voters. In particular, in the 2018 parliamentary elections, over 90% of Hungarians abroad voted for the pro-government FIDESZ (Sólymos, Finta, Cuprik, & Diko, 2021). Intriguing was the process of Hungary's efforts to win voters' preferences. In April 2010, the Hungarian parliament adopted the Hungarian citizenship law (a law that enables foreign Hungarians to obtain Hungarian citizenship under a simplified procedure)[38]. A few hours later, the National Council of the Slovak Republic responded with a mandatory requirement to renounce Slovak citi-

---

38 To obtain citizenship, it was not necessary to permanently reside in Hungary. It sufficed to be proficient in Hungarian or have Hungarian relatives.

zenship in the case of obtaining Hungarian citizenship (Maďaři schválili..., 2010). Recently, against the warming relations between Bratislava and Budapest, the countries have taken steps to renew the institution of dual citizenship in Slovakia. However, the Slovak Republic bans dual citizenship, and revising specialized laws would sooner lead to contrarieties in Slovak-Czech relations than those of Slovak-Hungarian (Körbl, 2022). However, since April 2022, further changes to the institute of Slovak citizenship, which affect Slovak-Hungarian relations, entered into force. First, upon acquiring citizenship of another state, a person does not lose Slovak citizenship on condition of continuous living outside the Slovak Republic for at least five years. The second modification is that the Slovaks who lost their citizenship because they had acquired citizenship of another country are entitled to the return of Slovak citizenship on condition of living abroad for five years (Parlament schválil novelu..., 2022).

During the Hungarian election campaigns, the tense relations between Budapest and Bratislava led to a paradoxical situation. On the one hand, foreign Hungarians living in Slovakia do not have the right to vote in Hungarian parliamentary elections because dual citizenship is not allowed in Slovakia. On the other hand, the Hungarian authorities had foreseen this situation and provided an option of online voting, permitting foreign Hungarians to vote remotely (2013. Évi XXXVI).

According to the most recent census, as of 2021, there was a minority of 422,065 Hungarians in Slovakia, an estimated 7.75% of the country's ethnic structure (Počet obyvateľov..., 2001). This is the largest ethnic minority in the Slovak Republic and one of the largest Hungarian minorities in the world. Most Hungarians live south and east of Slovakia along the border with Hungary. Since the first alternative parliamentary elections in 1990, the nearly 8% minority has steadily been represented in the parliament. The Hungarian minority would steadily win seats in the Slovak National Council, except for the last parliamentary elections in 2020, when either of the two most influential Hungarian parties (the more radical SMK-MKP and the more liberal MOST-HÍD) failed to pass the 5% voting barrier. Similarly, in early parliamentary elections in the autumn of 2023, the newly formed SZÖVETSÉG–ALIANCIA got only slightly more than 4% of the votes (Voľby a referendá).

Following the electoral fiasco in the 2020 parliamentary elections, Slovak Hungarians began a radical political rebranding to avoid gradually changing their political programme exclusively towards protecting the local interests of the Hungarian minority in the places of their compact residence. For Hungarian political parties, protecting the rights of Slovak Hungarians can be achieved only through parliamentary activities. For this purpose, in early October 2021, a new political force, SZÖVETSÉG–ALIANCIA, emerged, based on a political union of several influential political parties. As can be seen, they preserved bilingualism in the party name (Hungarian–Slovak). The experienced politician Krisztián Forró was elected party leader (Petrus, 2021).

Ideologically, SZÖVETSÉG–ALIANCIA is moderately pro-European; it aims to resolve existing conflicts and minimize potential Hungarian-Slovak conflicts. According to its political orientation, the party is right-centrist and national-conservative. It strategically pursues defending the interests of the Hungarian minority. However, it is not geographically confined to working with the Hungarian electorate solely in south and east Slovakia. The party prioritizes parliamentary activities. SZÖVETSÉG–ALIANCIA declares openness to political dialogue, except for cooperation with Robert Fico and Marian Kotleba, which is impossible (Petrus, 2021). The political tension arose from the Hungarian minority's complicated relations with Fico's 2010 government and the anti-Hungarian appeals of the right-wing radical Kotleba. Despite maintaining priority in the parliamentary electoral competition, the party pursues regionalism. One way or another, the Hungarian minority party's primary focus is solving problems in the south and east of the country. At the international level, SZÖVETSÉG–ALIANCIA cultivates international cooperation in the format of the Visegrad Four and the EU-8, which makes it close to Budapest. At the level of European politics, the party identifies with the liberal conservatives from the EPP (Strana Aliancia).

SZÖVETSÉG–ALIANCIA's first electoral experience was the October 2022 regional elections. In general, the newly formed party of the Hungarian minority succeeded and received the seats of the Regional Assemblies in "their districts". For comparison, at the national level, the Hungarians became the first political party that received 54 seats (12.88%) and lost only to independent candidates

– 159 seats (37.94%) (Voľby a referendá). The party was sure to lead in the areas of compact Hungarian residence, proved by the fact that they got 54 of the 94 possible seats in the "Hungarian regions" (primarily, the south and east of Slovakia) (see Table 10).

Table 10. Political Distribution of the Hungarian Minority at the Regional Level (according to the results of the 2022 regional elections in the Slovak Republic)[39].

Region (Kraj)	District (Okres)	Share of Hungarian Minority (%)	Seats Obtained by SZÖVETSÉG–ALIANCIA / Total Number of Seats in the Voting Districts
Bratislava	Senec; Electoral district No. 22[40]	9.01[41]	1/1
Trnava	Dunajská Streda	68.65	8/8
	Galanta	31.1	6/7
Nitra	Komárno	61.58	7/8
	Levice	31.1	5/9
	Nové Zámky, Electoral district No. 4[42]	31.89[43]	0/8
	Nové Zámky, Electoral district No. 6[44]	31.89	3/3
	Šaľa	27.94	3/4
Banská Bystrica region	Lučenec	23.54	2/5
	Revúca	19.02	1/3
	Rimavská Sobota	39.53	5/6
	Veľký Krtíš	21.44	1/3
Košice region	Košice-okolie	8.1	2/9
	Michalovce	10.44	0/8
	Rožňava	22.85	3/4
	Trebišov	24.14	7/8
Trenčín region		0.15	–

39 The distribution of the Hungarian ethnic minority in a particular district is not less than 5%.
40 The northeastern part of the Senec district without the town of Senec.
41 The figures are provided for the entire Senec area.
42 Most of the Nové Zámky district.
43 The figures are provided for the entire Nové Zámky area.
44 The southeastern part of the Nové Zámky district, with the centre in the town of Štúrovo.

Žilina region		0.09	–
Prešov region		0.1	–
Total			54 (57.44%)/94

Source: The author's calculations are based on the 2021 national census of the Slovak Republic and data from the Statistical Office of the Slovak Republic (Počet obyvateľov..., 2021; Voľby a referendá).

If we look into the electoral gains of SZÖVETSÉG–ALIANCIA in the Hungarian-populated districts, we can observe that Slovak Hungarians demonstrate high electoral activity. In the Dunajská Streda district, the Hungarian party gained all the seats. The Galanta district closely follows, with only one-third of the population being ethnic Hungarians (seven out of eight seats), or the Eastern district of Trebišov, with a quarter of ethnic Hungarians (also seven out of eight deputies are from SZÖVETSÉG–ALIANCIA). Even in the Bratislava region, the territorial peculiarities of voting district formation resulted in the Hungarian minority receiving one seat in the Bratislava Regional Assembly. On the other hand, the district of Nové Zámky, with one-third of the Hungarian minority, received an electoral maximum of three out of three seats in one voting district and none in the other. Interestingly, there are situations when the voting district coincides with the area of residence of ethnic Hungarians. However, the Michalovce district has a registered Hungarian minority of more than 10%, but SZÖVETSÉG–ALIANCIA failed to get a single seat in the Košice Regional Assembly. In general, social populist parties got support in one of the most conservative voting districts in the farthermost east of Slovakia (see Figure 8)[45].

The 2022 regional elections proved that Slovak regions are highly fragmented in terms of "Slovak politics vs Hungarian minority" cleavage. Pursuant to this cleavage, the following three groups of regions in the Slovak Republic can be outlined:

---

45 Most votes were cast for independent candidates or SMER-SD (in coalition with conservatives SME RODINA), traditionally strong in the country's far east: three deputies from each political force. The centre-right SaS and Progresívne Slovensko received only one seat; the HLAS-SD got a similar result.

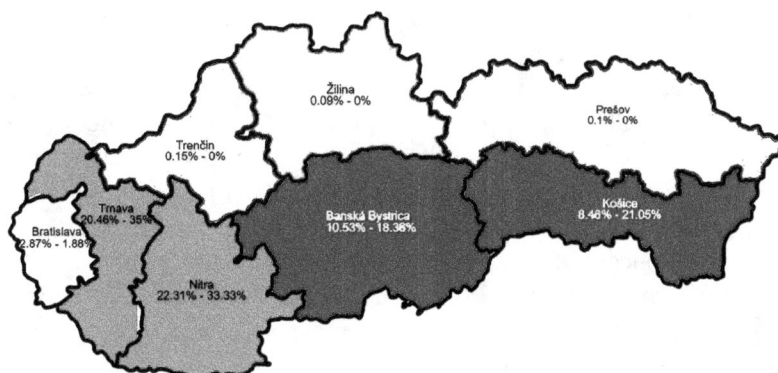

Figure 8. Fragmentation of the Slovak Regions According to the Political Cleavage "Slovak Politics vs Hungarian minority" (results of the 2022 regional elections)[46].

Source: the author's calculations are based on data from the Statistical Office of the Slovak Republic (Voľby a referendá).

(1) Highly fragmented regions: the SZÖVETSÉG–ALIANCIA party wins by the number of seats gained. These are the Slovak regions with the most considerable Hungarian ethnic minority, such as the Nitra and Trnava regions. In the Nitra region, the party of Hungarians won. In the Trnava region, they got the same number of parliamentary seats as independent candidates (14 deputies each), ranking first and second in the electoral race. Voting for a Župan displays high fragmentation in both regions. In the Trnava region, the incumbent Župan Jozef Viskupič had a rival, József Berényi, from SZÖVETSÉG–ALIANCIA[47]. Viskupič was elected Župan for the second term, but Berényi won in the two districts with the largest number of ethnic Hungarians.

Likewise, in the Nitra region, a candidate for Župan from SZÖVETSÉG–ALIANCIA, Tibor Csenger, ended up in a similar situation[48]. "The Hungarian candidate" lost 5% to Milan Belica (16.65%

---

46 Numerical values: first, the share of the Hungarian minority in the region is given; the second numerical value is the number of votes received by those loyal to SZÖVETSÉG–ALIANCIA.

47 József Berényi is an experienced politician who is affiliated with SMK-MKP. He successfully built a parliamentary career over a long time, having serious electoral support from the Hungarian ethnic minority.

48 His political career is closely related to the party of the Hungarian ethnic minority MKÖ-MKS.

vs 21.85%) but won in southern districts of the Nitra region with the highest Hungarian minority.

(2) Moderately fragmented regions. In regions where SZÖVET-SÉG–ALIANCIA came second, the political landscape is moderately fragmented. Two such regions are Banská Bystrica and Košice, which are quite large. The Hungarian minority is concentrated in the southern areas of these regions, near the border with Hungary. The percentage of Hungarian voters fluctuates between 8% and 10% in national indicators. In both Banská Bystrica and Košice regions, approximately one in five voters supported the party of the Hungarian minority.

In both the Banská Bystrica and Košice regions, the impact of the Hungarian minority on the ethnic structure was relatively low. As a result, the support for Župan candidates varied between the two regions. For instance, none of the candidates from SZÖVET-SÉG–ALIANCIA were registered in the Banská Bystrica region. However, in the Košice region, Rastislav Trnka, who was running as part of a centre-right polycoalition consisting of five political entities (including SZÖVETSÉG–ALIANCIA), won a clear victory (55.31%) for the second time in a row. Therefore, the Hungarian ethnic minority had minimal influence on the election of Župan in both regions.

(3) Non-fragmented regions are regions where the political party SZÖVETSÉG–ALIANCIA did not receive any seats, and the number of Hungarian ethnic minorities ranges from 0% to 2%. The only exception to this is the Bratislava region, where one of the voting districts (No. 22) with the highest number of ethnic Hungarians elected one deputy. Also, it is important to note that only one deputy seat was allocated specifically to this district as per the maximum electoral quota. In the regions of Trenčín, Žilina, and Prešov, the Hungarian ethnic minority had very little influence. However, to some extent, this division can be observed in the Prešov region, where the political group SZÖVETSÉG–ALIAN-CIA had some electoral presence[49]. In the Prešov region, Michal

---

49 In the Prešov region, SZÖVETSÉG–ALIANCIA formed a broad coalition with the two leading parties in the region, HLAS-SD and SMER-SD. Due to this, it is challenging to determine the number of voters who supported the Hungarian ethnic party. It is noteworthy that an "informal" political alliance between the

Kaliňák participated in the election for the position of Župan and secured 31.39% of the votes. He represented an unusual alliance of left-wing political parties, namely HLAS-SD, SMER-SD, and SZÖVETSÉG–ALIANCIA. It is worth noting that the leaders of the newly formed SZÖVETSÉG–ALIANCIA have stated their stance on not cooperating with Robert Fico.

In the 2020 parliamentary elections, the support for traditional ideological parties decreased significantly. This has led to independent candidates becoming the top leaders in the regional elections. Following these independent candidates, the only political party representing the Hungarian ethnic minority gained support. In the 2022 regional elections, SZÖVETSÉG–ALIANCIA finished second overall in the number of votes and became the leader among all competing political entities (parties/coalitions). Therefore, the issue of the Hungarian ethnic minority factor, which seemed to have fallen in the 2020 parliamentary elections, became a topic of discussion once again. The Slovak Republic is home to a Hungarian minority which constitutes 7.75% of the population. In the recent elections, this minority managed to secure 12.88% of the seats in the parliament through their own political party, SZÖVETSÉG–ALIANCIA. The party is made up of both new and experienced politicians, mostly from the previous SMK-MKP political format, who have been actively working to build support in the electoral field of certain south and east regions of the Slovak Republic. The key factor behind the success of SZÖVETSÉG–ALIANCIA was their effective political rebranding of the broader political movement of ethnic Hungarians in Slovakia. A new political party emerged from the combination of the most influential Hungarian political parties in the south and east of the country: SMK-MKP, MOST-HÍD, and MKÖ-MKS. This party became the hope for the future of the Hungarian minority in the region. In the 2022 regional elections, the Hungarian minority expressed their political dissatisfaction with the traditional Hungarian political parties by voting for the new SZÖVETSÉG–ALIANCIA party. However, the early 2023 parliamentary elections showed that there was a difference be-

---

ethnic Hungarian party and Robert Fico's force was tested at the regional level. This contradicts the statements made by the leader of SZÖVETSÉG–ALIANCIA, Krisztián Forró, in autumn 2021.

tween national and regional elections for the Hungarian minority party. Unfortunately, SZÖVETSÉG–ALIANCIA failed to pass the 5% barrier.

SZÖVETSÉG–ALIANCIA is a political party that follows a pro-European ideology and maintains a balanced cooperation strategy with the capital city of Bratislava. The party embraces traditional Hungarian values and promotes Christian democracy, while managing a balance between the Hungarian autonomism of the MKÖ-MKS and the "moderate" liberalism of the MOST-HÍD. With its new approach, SZÖVETSÉG–ALIANCIA aims to represent the entire Hungarian ethnic minority, while also attracting the liberal-conservative Slovak voter. It is important to consider the impact of Hungarian politics on Hungarians living abroad. This includes the influence of Prime Minister Viktor Orbán, who has a long history of in Hungarian politics. SZÖVETSÉG–ALIANCIA is a political party that represents the interests of the Hungarian minority in Slovak politics, but in order to do so, it must maintain a relationship with Budapest. Despite party leader Krisztián Forró's attempts to distance himself from Prime Minister Orbán, there have been accusations that SZÖVETSÉG–ALIANCIA receives financial support from Budapest[50]. Objectively, Viktor Orbán's political influence will be reflected in any influential party of the Hungarian minority in modern Slovakia.

In the early parliamentary elections of autumn 2023, Robert Fico's political revenge slightly shifted the political landscape of the "Slovak politics vs Hungarian minority" cleavage. Although Fico and Orbán's political relationship has improved and seems like an alliance, it is unlikely to erase the electoral divide between the Slovaks and Hungarian ethnic minorities. Fico's return to the prime minister's chair saw him use openly populist and conservative appeals that included anti-Western and pro-Russian rhetoric. After running a pre-election program focused on criticizing the EU and the West as instruments of government policy, Robert Fico was re-elected to office in Slovakia. Following his inauguration, Fico continued to maintain analogies with his Hungarian counterpart, Viktor Orbán, through his rhetoric of preserving Slovak interests

---

50 The aforementioned journalistic investigations were disseminated several months ahead of the 2022 regional elections (Kniš, 2022).

in Europe. This rhetoric includes departing from the foundations of European social democracy, criticizing the EU using legal populism, and refusing to aid Ukraine in its resistance against Russia's military aggression. Despite his rhetoric, R. Fico supports most European initiatives in practice and tries to act universally (Slovenskí politici..., 2022). In the last election, the Hungarian minority party SZÖVETSÉG–ALIANCIA failed to enter the parliament, receiving only 4.38% of the votes, while Robert Fico and Viktor Orbán's relationship improved (Voľby a referendá). It is highly probable that the recent electoral defeat of the Hungarian party will further deepen the electoral cleavage of the Hungarian ethnic minority.

3.3 Political Cleavage "Party vs Independent Deputies"

Independent candidates are playing an increasingly important role in the electoral processes of the Slovak Republic. The political institute of independent candidates has undergone successful testing at both the local level, including regional and local elections, and partially in national politics, such as presidential elections. Notably, during the autumn regional elections of 2022, the number of independent deputies reached a historic high, surpassing that of party deputies. Consequently, the "independents vs party deputies" political cleavage became increasingly apparent during several regional election campaigns in the Slovak Republic. This cleavage at the regional level can be explained from several perspectives.

The introduction of independent deputies in post-socialist Slovakia has posed a challenge to political crises and has aimed to explain the general decline in the legitimacy of traditional political parties and their leaders. This phenomenon has been particularly noteworthy in the context of the political crisis that took place during Vladimír Mečiar's premiership in the late 1990s, which was marked by a political cleavage between Mečiarism and anti-Mečiarism. Similarly, the murder of investigative journalist Ján

Kuciak has led to a deep political crisis that is distinguished by the Fico–anti-Fico cleavage (Haydanka, 2021a). In both instances, the voters of Slovakia demonstrated their proclivity towards seeking out and ultimately endorsing alternative candidates. During the parliamentary elections in 1998, the poly-ideological anti-Mečiar coalition received support from the electorate. This trend was further reinforced by the election of Rudolf Schuster, who was "partially" independent, in the first national presidential elections in 1999[51]. The impact of independent candidates in the election of the President in the years 2014 and 2019 cannot be disregarded. In 2014, the independent candidate Andrej Kiska emerged victorious, while five years later, Zuzana Čaputová, an independent and progressive candidate, also claimed the position of President.

The political fragmentation of regions in modern Slovakia has remained a persistent factor over time. Conservative parties such as the "people's" party HZDS, led by Vladimír Mečiar in the 1990s, or social populists such as the SMER-SD led by Robert Fico in the 2000s, have traditionally enjoyed significant support from voters in the eastern regions. In contrast, the western part of Slovakia, particularly the Bratislava region, has tended to lean towards more liberal party ideologies. For instance, the SDKÚ in the late 1990s to early 2010s, SaS in 2016, and Progresívne Slovensko in the early parliamentary elections in 2023 have all enjoyed notable support from voters in this region. The political spectrum of the contemporary Slovak Republic is highly diverse. Despite the onset of a severe political crisis in early December 2022, as many as nine political parties managed to garner electoral support exceeding 5%. This information underscores the importance of understanding the complexities of Slovakia's political landscape and the various factors that shape it[52]. In the years 2022–2023, Peter Pellegrini, a member of the extra-parliamentary HLAS-SD Party, received a significant level of electoral support, exceeding 20% (Voľby a referendá). However, during this period, the government coalition

---

51 Rudolf Schuster, backed by a broad coalition anti-Mečiar coalition, emphasized the importance of supporting independent deputies in his election program (Haydanka, 2021b, pp. 22–23).
52 HLAS-SD, SMER-SD, Progresívne Slovensko, SME RODINA, OĽaNO, REPUBLIKA, KDH, SaS, SZÖVETSÉG–ALIANCIA.

in the parliament collapsed, leading to the resignation of Eduard Heger's government by the end of 2022. This event exposed the diversity of political parties in the country and the usual inability of Slovak politicians to reach a consensus during crisis times. Unfortunately, the pro-European parliamentary coalition was unable to continue working together due to Robert Fico's political revenge in the first half of 2023. Despite the early parliamentary elections in the autumn of 2023 and the appointment of a new premiership of Robert Fico, the level of electoral fragmentation in Slovakia has remained high. As of November 2023, nine different political parties have garnered at least 5% of the national vote [Volebné preferencie..., 2002–2023]. With the country's regions becoming increasingly politically fragmented and the leaders of leading parties being delegitimized along the "west–east" line, independent candidates are emerging as a viable political alternative.

The regional elections in the Slovak Republic are closely associated with the participation of independent candidates. In accordance with the current election laws, independent candidates are recognized as active participants in the electoral processes at the regional level. The Law "On Elections to Bodies of Self-Governing Regions" of 2001 specifies that candidates can be nominated for Regional Assemblies on the lists of political parties or as independent candidates (§14, 1). Similarly, candidates for the position of Župan can be nominated by a political party or a group of parties, or as an independent candidate (§19, 1) (Zákon č. 302/2001). As per the current electoral trends, independent candidates are gaining notable support from voters. In the first regional elections held in 2001, independent candidates were more of an experimental concept. However, in the more recent 2017 and 2022 elections, the majority of voters opted to vote for independent candidates as opposed to candidates affiliated with political parties (see Table 11).

During the last six election campaigns, the number of independents elected to the Regional Assemblies grew significantly. Moreover, the overall level of electoral support for independent candidates increased several times. In the 2022 elections, one-third of the voters cast their votes for independent candidates. However, in the previous elections of 2017, the support for independent candidates reached a record of nearly 40% of the votes. The degree of fragmentation of the regional level by the criterion of electoral

Table 11. Electoral Support for Independent Candidates in Regional Elections in the Slovak Republic (2001–2022).

Election year	Independent Candidates (% seats)	Region with Largest Number of Independent Candidates (%)	Regions Without Independent Candidates
2001	4.48	Košice (14.03)	Trnava region, Trenčín region, Nitra region
2005	9.46	Prešov (19.35)	Nitra region
2009	13.48	Košice (22.8)	–
2013	17.89	Žilina (28.07)	–
2017	39.4	Žilina / Bratislava (25)	–
2022	37.94	Žilina (52)	–

Source: the author's calculations are based on the Statistical Office of the Slovak Republic (Voľby a referendá).

support for independent candidates is determined by the insignificant interest of "independent politicians" in the western regions, and to a lesser extent in the Bratislava region. In the east, specifically in the regions of Prešov and Košice, independent candidates have received significant support since the first regional elections in 2001. It is noteworthy that in the northern Žilina region, independent candidates have consistently been the leaders in terms of the number of elected deputies for three consecutive election campaigns (2013, 2017, and 2022). To determine the level of political fragmentation in Slovak regions, the degree of electoral support that independent candidates and political parties/blocs received in the 2022 elections will be analysed (see Figure 9).

In regions with a low level of influence of independent candidates, the electoral support ranges from 20% to 30%. This group includes three Western Slovak regions – the Bratislava, Trnava, and Nitra regions. Notably, in the Bratislava region, where the best party result was 50.94% and the result of independent deputies was 24.52%, more than half of the seats went to the centre-right coalition of the "presidential" party Progresívne Slovensko, the liberal conservatives SaS, and the local Team Bratislava. The results of

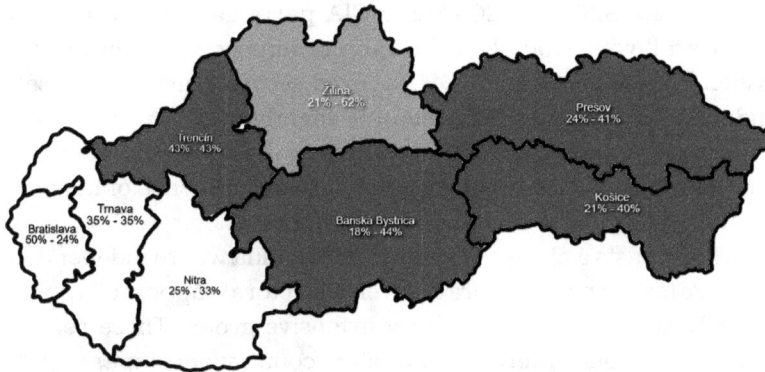

Figure 9. The Structure of the Regional Assemblies of the Slovak Republic in 2022 Based on the Political Cleavage between Independent Candidates and Party Deputies[53].

Source: the author's calculations are based on the Statistical Office of the Slovak Republic (Voľby a referendá).

the recent election in Bratislava indicate a notable level of trust in non-mainstream parties and local political forces. The third-place finish of the party of Slovak towns and villages, "SOM Slovensko", demonstrates the significant support these groups garnered. Furthermore, only one in four voters in the capital region opted for independent deputies, suggesting that pro-liberal sentiments and non-mainstream voting were prevalent in the Bratislava region. In the Trnava region, both party deputies and independent candidates have emerged as leaders with an equal share of 35% each. Furthermore, the newly formed SZÖVETSÉG–ALIANCIA party has secured an impressive 14 seats, which is proportional to the number of seats won by independent candidates, highlighting a noteworthy electoral cleavage between Slovak politics and the Hungarian minority. The main competition for the top two positions was between the centre-right coalition, which had a diverse ideological composition ranging from KDH to OĽaNO. In the West Slovak region of Nitra (33.33% / 20.37%), the Hungarian ethnic minority demonstrated a notable impact on the recent election. Spe-

---

53 The numerical values indicate the largest share of seats the party/coalition received in the Regional Assemblies. The second numerical value represents the number of seats received by independent candidates of the Regional Assembly.

cifically, the SZÖVETSÉG–ALIANCIA party garnered a third of the overall vote. Notably, a coalition of nine centre-right parties, which included SaS and KDH, secured second place. Conversely, independent deputies received only slightly over 20% of the vote, thus ranking last among the top three. It is also pertinent to note that the Nitra region demonstrated the least influence of independent deputies in the broader context of the nation.

There exists a cluster of regions in Slovakia where independent candidates garner an average level of electoral support of approximately 40%, making it the most extensive group. These regions span across four different areas of the country, encompassing the north, centre, and east. The situation in the Trenčín region (43.18% / 43.18%) is analogous to that in the Trnava region, where a coalition of social democrats and conservatives share leadership with independent deputies. In the Trenčín region, supporters of Robert Fico, Peter Pellegrini, and independent candidates share political influence.

In the Banská Bystrica region (18.36% / 44.89%), although being in the group with average support of independent deputies, the actual electoral dominance lies with the latter. SZÖVETSÉG–ALIANCIA, the party of the Hungarian minority, came in second after the independent deputies with a result two and a half times smaller. The party received a little more than 18% of the total votes. After that, the traditional Slovak right-wing and centre-left parties received only minor support. This clearly demonstrates the indisputable electoral dominance of independent deputies in the region.

In the eastern region of Slovakia, the number of independent candidates outnumbers the competing parties by twice the margin. In the Prešov region (24.61% / 41.53%), both centre-left and centre-right parties have an equal number of mandates, accounting for half of the total mandates. Similarly, in the nearby Košice region (21.05% / 40.35%), the party of Hungarians SZÖVETSÉG–ALIANCIA was the second most popular choice. Other political parties failed to secure a significant political representation.

The Žilina region has been the only region where independent candidates managed to obtain a majority in the Regional Assembly, with a 21.05% / 52.63% split. This has resulted in the formation of a group of independent candidates, who have demonstrated a high level of influence. The Social Democrats and the Christian

Democrats both lost significantly to the independent candidates, with the rest of the political parties securing only one to two mandates. Overall, this indicates the desire of local voters to seek "new faces" in politics, including within their region.

The analysis of the role of independent candidates in the election of Regional Župans reveals a distinct contrast with the composition of the Regional Assemblies. The 2022 elections witnessed only one independent candidate out of the eight possible Župans being elected. Nonetheless, the candidate's electoral status at the time of the election, their prior political (party) experience, and their involvement in Slovak politics are all pertinent considerations. It is noteworthy that the position of Župans is often combined with the position of a deputy in the National Council. This study will provide a comprehensive insight into the political backgrounds of the Župans who were elected in the 2022 regional elections.

Jaroslav Baška, a newly elected Župan and a seasoned and highly experienced politician, has demonstrated exceptional electoral performance as a member of the SMER-SD Party in the Trenčín region. Baška has been elected to the National Council five times consecutively, beginning in 2002, and most recently in the early elections of 2023. His political career has been closely associated with SMER-SD, and his achievements in this regard are noteworthy (Voľby a referendá). Jaroslav Baška, a member of the SMER-SD Party, was first elected as the Župan of the Trenčín region in 2013. He subsequently won re-election for a second term in 2017. Baška's tenure exemplifies the limited rotation of political elites in the region. His long-term service as Župan has afforded him a strong foothold in the region, enabling him to maintain his position and provide SMER-SD with a seat in one of the most electorally stable regions for Robert Fico.

Juraj Droba, a well-respected politician in Slovakia, was elected in 2022 as the Župan in the Bratislava region. It is noteworthy that there was not a single independent candidate among the eight registered candidates. Droba faced considerably less competition and was able to secure 63.6% of the votes. The runner-up, a candidate from SMER-SD and SNS, only received 13.4% of the votes. Droba is a seasoned politician who has been repeatedly elected to the National Council since 2010 (Voľby a referendá). He has maintained a close relationship with the SaS Party, collaborating with them in various capacities, such as co-founding and leaving it (Poslanec Juraj Droba..., 2014). Since 2017, he has focused on gaining leadership at the regional level and was elected Župan of the Bratislava region for the first time. He won the regional elections in 2022 and became the Župan for the second consecutive term. Droba's political orientation is liberal, which is evident from the fact that he contested the elections from a trio of ideologically moderate parties – SaS, Progresívne Slovensko, and TEAM Bratislava. His victory in the elections is a testament to the pro-liberal sentiments of the capital's voters and highlights the lack of need for independent candidates for higher positions in the region. In the early parliamentary elections of 2023, he was elected to the parliament from SaS, a testament to his growing political influence and popularity.

Rastislav Trnka, the recently elected Župan in the Košice region, has achieved an absolute majority of votes, marking another significant success in his political career. As a traditional politician, Trnka has demonstrated a strong commitment to local and regional self-government, with little interest in pursuing a career at the national level. Notably, he became the youngest Župan in the country in 2017, marking a significant achievement in his already impressive political journey. Widely regarded as a mainstream and independent politician, Trnka actively collaborated with SDKÚ-DS in 2010 and SIEŤ in 2013, further showcasing his political abilities and dedication (Trnka, 2024). In the regional elections held in 2022, Trnka was nominated by a diverse range of political parties, including the Christian Democrats and the party of Hungarians. He enjoyed a comfortable victory, as his closest competitor secured only 15% of the total votes. Notably, independent candidates were only able to secure a maximum of 6% of the votes, indicating that Trnka had successfully taken over the independent candidate's "electoral niche". It is worth mentioning that Trnka is one of two acting Župans who did not participate in the parliamentary elections held in the autumn of 2023.

The following passage discusses the group of Župans, who managed to garner electoral support ranging from 30% to 40%. Among these candidates, the sole independent candidate who emerged triumphant in the mayoral elections was Ondrej Lunter, who recorded the highest number of votes. Lunter is a young and promising politician who ascended to the position of Župan at the

age of 35, taking over from his father, Ján Lunter. He was successfully elected as the Župan of the Banská Bystrica region (Lunter,
2024). This a clear case when the position of Župan is passed down
from father to son and reflects its dynastic nature. However, Ondrej Lunter was able to establish an independent pre-election
programme that set him apart from any political party, based
on his high level of professionalism as a regional leader. His programme was highly successful in mobilizing the electorate, thanks
to his comprehensive development program for the Central Slovak region, which he titled "Together we will achieve the most"[54]
(Lunter, 2022). In the regional elections held in 2022, Ondrej Lunter
emerged as an undisputable victor, winning by a substantial margin over his competitors. The second-place candidate was also an
independent, but with only 15% of the votes, lagging significantly
behind the leader. Ondrej Lunter was one of only two Župans out
of eight who chose not to contest the 2023 parliamentary elections.
This decision reflects his unwavering commitment to remain independent and distance himself from political parties, with a focus
solely on resolving the region's issues.

Milan Majerský was re-elected as Župan for the second consecutive time in the Eastern Slovak Prešov region. Majerský is an
esteemed politician in the area, with conservative views that are
particularly favoured in the eastern part of the country. His political achievements are local in nature and were accomplished during his tenure as the mayor of Levoča, a town with a population of
nearly 15,000 people (Voľby a referendá). Majerský has been successfully elected as the Župan of the Prešov region twice in a row
since 2017 with the supportive backing of the Christian Democrats.
He has made a gradual ascent to the highest positions of regional
self-government. In the latest regional elections of 2022, Milan Majerský astoundingly won over 10% of the vote, triumphing over the
representative of the "pro-Fico" forces. However, independent candidates failed to make any significant impact in the Prešov region,
as the voters only supported them at a meagre level of 3–4%. Majerský has been focusing on his party career since 2020 and has
even been elected as the chairman of the KDH (Zaslúžite…, 2024).
He was able to effectively combine both regional and party leader-

---

54 Slov.: *"Spoločne dokážeme najviac"*.

ship, resulting in a successful election to the National Council in the early parliamentary elections of 2023. Majerský is a politician who emphasizes a clear party ideology, with Christian democracy being his chosen focus.

In the Trnava region of Western Slovakia, Jozef Viskupič was elected to serve as Župan for a second consecutive term. Prior to this appointment, Viskupič commenced his political career with SaS and later moved to Igor Matovič's OĽaNO political project. He has consistently been voted to the National Council. Most recently he represented OĽaNO and obtained a seat in the 2023 parliamentary elections. Viskupič is regarded as a forward-thinking politician, having previous experience as a project manager, which has contributed to his positive image within the political sphere (Osobný profil..., 2023). In 2017, Jozef Viskupič's progressive views and alignment with "new faces" in politics were validated when he replaced Tibor Mikuš as Župan of the Trnava region. Mikuš, who had served as Župan for three consecutive terms, was associated with conservative Mečiarist politics. This rotation in leadership solidified Viskupič's position as a forward-thinking and innovative political figure in the region (Voľby a referendá). In the regional elections of 2022, Viskupič emerged as the clear winner, successfully defeating his opponents who received support ranging from 11% to 20% of the electoral votes. It is worth noting that the distribution of votes amongst the competitors was quite even. Additionally, an independent candidate with significant influence was able to secure over 16% of the total votes cast.

In the Žilina region of Slovakia, the re-election bid of Erika Jurinová as Župan was met with underwhelming results, with only one-third of voters in the region supporting her second term. Jurinová is a seasoned politician with extensive experience, having been elected three times to the National Council of the Slovak Republic since 2010. She began her political career working alongside the SaS and later co-founded OĽaNO (Voľby a referendá). In 2017, Jurinová made history by becoming the first female Župan in the Slovak Republic. In 2018, two acting Župans from OĽaNO, Jozef Viskupič from Trnava and Erika Jurinová from Žilina, relinquished their mandates in the National Council, which looked rather populist. After serving two years as Deputies of Parliament, both individuals expressed their desire to focus on working in their respective regions (Jurinová a Viskupič..., 2018). In the regional elections of 2022, Jurinová emerged victorious with a significant lead of over 10% of the vote, surpassing her two competitors from SMER-SD and the centre-right coalition with KDH. Independent candidates, on the other hand, received a minimal amount of electoral support, garnering only 2–3% of the votes. In the subsequent early parliamentary elections of 2023, Jurinová was reelected to the parliament from OĽaNO.

Branislav Becík, from the Nitra region, was able to secure the position of Župan despite a relatively low electoral index of 27.49%. The situation in the Nitra region regarding the permanence of Župan is comparable to that of the Trnava region. Between 2001 and 2022, Milan Belica was the only individual to have been elected as Župan of the Nitra region. He spent a total of 21 consecutive years in the highest regional post. Being a typical old-school politician, Milan Belica first ran for office from Mečiar's HZDS and then pursued his career as a member of SMER-SD (Belica, 2009). In the 2022 regional elections, several candidates emerged as viable alternatives to the long-serving Župan. Belica, who participated in the elections as an independent candidate for the first time, secured second place. Becík was elected as a candidate from HLAS-SD. The newly elected Župan has emphasized the need to address the existing problems of the region swiftly. He has portrayed himself as a successful farmer who aims to transform the Nitra region into a thriving agricultural centre (Becík, 2024). In 2023, Becík, who is a member of the HLAS-SD Party, was elected to serve as a member of parliament. Despite his parliamentary duties, he decided to also take on the responsibility of Župan.

In brief, the institute of independent deputies appears to hold an equivocal position in the Slovak Republic. As of the 2022 regional elections, independent candidates secured more than 37% of mandates in the Regional Assemblies, with every third MP being independent. These results indicate a persistent crisis of traditional ideologies endorsed by major Slovak parties and a growing inclination to support regional non-mainstream leaders. However, it is noteworthy that only one out of the eight Župans is independent, while the rest belong to different political parties or coalitions. In the early elections of 2023, six out of eight Župans were elected to the parliament. This suggests that certain political forces in the re-

Table 12. Political and Party Affiliation of the Newly Elected Župans (based on the 2022 regional elections).

Region	Župan (% result)	Candidature Nomination	Party Affiliation on the Eve of the 2022 Elections
Bratislava	Juraj Droba (63.60)	SaS, Progresívne Slovensko, Team Bratislava	MP of the National Council – SaS, 2020
Trnava	Jozef Viskupič (38.56)	Broad coalition led by OĽaNO	MP of the National Council – OĽaNO, 2016
Nitra	Branislav Becík (27.49)	Bipartisan coalition HLAS-SD – SME RODINA	Candidate for the National Council – Dobrá voľba, 2020
Banská Bystrica	Ondrej Lunter (47.53)	Independent candidate with party support [55]	none
Košice	Rastislav Trnka (51.31)	A broad coalition led by KDH	Župan of the Košice region 2017 – independent candidate with party support [56]
Trenčín	Jaroslav Baška (67.25)	A broad four-subject coalition [57]	MP of the National Council – SMER-SD, 2020
Žilina	Erika Jurinová (32.04)	A broad coalition led by OĽaNO	Župan of the Žilina region 2017 – independent candidate with party support [58]
Prešov	Milan Majerský (42.01)	A broad four-subject coalition [59]	Župan of the Prešov region 2017 – four-subject coalition [60]

Source: the author's calculations are based on the Statistical Office of the Slovak Republic (Voľby a referendá).

gion may have engaged in "electoral lobbying", which could be reflected in the results of the parliamentary elections (see Table 13). This is particularly noteworthy as the majority of the Župans were re-elected for a second term in their respective regions.[55][56][57][58][59][60]

---

55 SaS–KDH–Progresívne Slovensko–SPOLU–OKS–HLAS-SD
56 KDH–SaS–OĽaNO–NOVA–ŠANCA
57 SMER-SD–HLAS-SD–SME RODINA–SNS
58 OĽaNO–SaS–KDH–OKS–NOVA
59 KDH–SME RODINA–SaS–ZA ĽUDÍ
60 KDH–OĽANO–SaS–NOVA

Table 13. The degree of "electoral lobbying" in the regions (based on the 2023 early parliamentary election outcome).

Region	Župan (Place on the Party List)	Party Affiliation / Votes Received by the Party in the Region / Party Rating in the Region	Party Votes Received Throughout the Country (%) / Party Rating Throughout the Country / Region (Best Indicator)
Bratislava	Juraj Droba (8)	SaS / 12.50% / 3rd place	6.32 / 6th place / Bratislava region
Trnava	Jozef Viskupič (5)	OĽaNO / 9.40% / 5th place	8.89 / 4th place/ Prešov region
Nitra	Branislav Becík (7)	HLAS-SD / 14.40% / 3rd place	14.70 / 3rd place / Banská Bystrica region
Banská Bystrica	Ondrej Lunter (-)	-	-
Košice	Rastislav Trnka[26] (-)	-	-
Trenčín	Jaroslav Baška (8)	SMER-SD / 29.47% / 1st place	22.94 / 1st place / Trenčín region
Žilina	Erika Jurinová (1)	OĽaNO / 6.90% / 6th place	8.89 / 4th place / Prešov region
Prešov	Milan Majerský (1)	KDH / 14.07% / 4th place	6.82 / 5th place / Prešov region

Source: the author's calculations are based on the Statistical Office of the Slovak Republic (Voľby a referendá).

The evidence indicates that the hypothesis concerning Župan's alleged "electoral lobbying" of their parties in the regions is only partially accurate. Among the six Župans affiliated with political parties, only three were able to lead the regions in which their party achieved the best result in the last parliamentary elections of 2023. These Župans include Juraj Droba, who was ranked eighth on the SaS Party list in the 2023 parliamentary elections and currently serves as the Župan of Bratislava region. In the Bratislava region, SaS received twice as many votes as the national average. Similarly, Milan Majerský, who is the head of KDH, was elected to parliament as the party's number one on the party list and currently serves as the Župan of the Prešov region. KDH also received twice as many votes as the national average in the Prešov region. The Trenčín Župan, Jaroslav Baška, also belongs here, as the regional electoral results of SMER-SD in the region represented the party's best performance in the country. However, a different scenario was observed in the other three regions, all of which are led by party-affiliated Župans. In these regions, the party associated with Župans failed to achieve the top result. Instead, in the Trnava and Žilina regions, OĽaNO secured the fifth and sixth positions, respectively, while in the Nitra region, HLAS-SD achieved the third position. Overall, it appears that voters in the regions tend to support their regional leaders more than nationally dominant political parties.

Conclusions

The analysis of the results of the regional elections in the Slo-vak Republic has underscored the necessity for a more in-depth examination of electoral processes within the regions. The autono-my of regional authorities has become a vital factor in the Slovak Republic's alignment with the EU. The regional elections conduct-ed in the Slovak Republic between 2001 and 2022 also revealed the extent of political fragmentation across the regions. We endeav-our to delineate the primary patterns of political fragmentation in Slovak regions based on the outcomes of regional elections.

Between 1996 and 2001, the Slovak Republic established the necessary structures of its administrative-territorial system, rang-ing from regional to local self-government. Upon joining the EU in 2004, the European nomenclature of territorial organization was formally established. Subsequently, NUTS-3 level territories were allocated to regional self-government bodies, while LAU-2 level ter-ritories were allocated to local self-government bodies. This has fostered a more organized and efficient governance system for the Slovak Republic. Fiscal autonomy plays a crucial role in ensur-ing that regional and local communities have the necessary level of autonomy they require. Despite this, there is still a significant disparity in the level of regional GDP in the Slovak Republic. The Bratislava region exhibits high European indicators of GDP per capita, surpassing the national indicator of the Trnava region by a slight margin. However, the remaining regions have indicators below the country's average value of regional GDP per capita, ranging from 61% to 89%.

In 2001, the adoption of electoral legislation served to regulate the electoral processes in the regions, thereby solidifying the po-litical autonomy of regional authorities. It is crucial that both the Regional Assemblies and Župans are elected directly, emphasiz-ing the importance of qualitative representation. Prior to the 2017 elections, two-round voting was permissible, with the second round specifically addressing the election of Župans failing to secure the required 50% of votes. However, following the change in electoral legislation in 2014, the 2017 regional elections were conducted in a single round of voting. The electoral rule of a relative major-ity of votes was introduced for Župans. The recent 2022 elections were notably groundbreaking, as they combined regional and lo-cal elections on the same day.

The voter turnout in regional elections is notably lower than that observed in national elections (parliamentary and presidential) and local elections, although it surpasses the turnout in European elections. The average turnout for the six regional election campaigns conducted stands at 26.79%. The lowest recorded turnout was observed during the second regional elections in 2005, likely attributed to "voter fatigue" among Slovak voters. Conversely, the highest turnout was noted in the most recent elections in 2022, attributable to the electorate's participation in the election of regional and communal authorities. Notably, the Banská Bystrica region exhibits the highest voter activity, while the Bratislava and Košice regions demonstrate the lowest levels of voter engagement.

The regional elections conducted in 2001 provided evident proof of the successful implementation of political decentralization in Slovakia. The electoral processes in the regions significantly bolstered the political capacity of regional authorities and districts. The sustained political rivalry between the HZDS and anti-Mečiar forces, previously observed at the national level, extended to regional levels, resulting in noteworthy implications. Notably, the populist conservative HZDS, independently or through coalitions, secured victories in five out of eight regions. Conversely, the Bratislava and Eastern Slovak Košice regions experienced decisive wins for the anti-Mečiar forces. Moreover, the Nitra region witnessed a distinct triumph for the SMK-MKP, underscoring the active electoral participation of the Hungarian ethnic minority. The political struggle between HZDS and anti-Mečiar forces was also evident during Župan elections, which reflected the outcomes of the Regional Assemblies' member elections. HZDS representatives emerged victorious in six out of eight regions, either independently or as part of election coalitions with HZDS in Trnava, Nitra, Banská Bystrica, and Prešov regions. The success of HZDS was also evident in Nitra, where the party of the Hungarian coalition SMK-MKP secured the highest number of seats in the Regional Assembly. Additionally, representatives from centre-right and liberal political forces triumphed in the capital Bratislava region (Ľubomír Roman) and in the Kosice region (Rudolf Bauer). Consequently, the initial regional elections bolstered the positions of pro-Mečiar political forces in the regions, while anti-Mečiar political forces gained strength in the capital and the eastern regions of the Slovak Republic (Košice region).

The 2005 regional elections revealed distinct electoral patterns. The capital Bratislava region exhibited a clear preference for pro-government and liberal-conservative parties. The Christian Democrats (KDH) achieved solid results and successfully forged an alliance with the pro-government SDKÚ at the party level. An independent candidate and a prominent local politician emerged victorious in the Župan elections. The influence of SMER-SD, in coalition with conservative political forces, continued to expand. Furthermore, representatives from SMER-SD took the lead in the north, centre, and entire east of the Slovak Republic. In addition, three regions elected representatives from the conservative-populist ĽS-HZDS as Župan. The practice of re-electing Župans, exemplified by Milan Belica in the Nitra region and Peter Chudík in the Prešov region, was established subsequent to the 2005 regional elections.

The outcomes of the 2009 regional elections underscored enduring electoral trends. Firstly, a distinct electoral cleavage between the western and eastern regions emerged, with the former supporting the pro-government centre-right coalition of SDKÚ-DS–KDH, and the latter favouring the populist conservatives ĽS-HZDS–SMER. Notably, SMER-SD succeeded in winning the Košice region without the need for electoral coalitions. Secondly, the electoral strategy of forging a poly-ideological electoral coalition in the Nitra region, uniting right-wing and left-wing political forces, was upheld, seemingly to contend for political influence alongside the Hungarian minority party SMK-MKP. Lastly, the proportion of independent deputies elected to the Regional Assemblies is on the rise. In the 2009 regional elections, independent deputies accounted for 13.44% of all mandates (55 out of 408). In the 2009 regional elections, significant differences were observed in the selection of regional leaders (Župans) when compared to previous elections. Notably, half of the Župans were elected in the first round, indicating a high level of legitimacy for the heads of regions. In the context of Slovak regional politics, individual Župans eventually formed their "own" regions. It is worth noting that two out of eight Župans were elected for the third time, four for the second time, and only in the regions of Bratislava and Banská Bystrica were new Župans elected. Additionally, parliamentary elections were anticipated in the Slovak Republic within six months, which could potentially indicate political allegiance to the central offices of the parties of the heads of the Regional Assemblies.

In the 2013 regional elections, SMER-SD established its political dominance at the level of the Regional Assemblies, securing victories in five out of eight regions. Furthermore, the social democrats formed electoral coalitions with the christian democrats of the KDH in the Nitra and Banská Bystrica regions, despite their ideological differences. These coalitions yielded significant electoral results, garnering the largest number of votes in both regions. Notably, the Bratislava region exhibited an electoral distancing from other Slovak regions, with two-thirds of Bratislava voters supporting the centre-right coalition. Regarding the positions of Župans, a similar situation has arisen, with five Župans being representatives of SMER-SD. The continuity of political incumbency in the post of Župan is evident, as six Župans have been re-elected for the second, third, or fourth consecutive term. In regions such as Nitra and Prešov, the same candidates have held office since 2001. Consequently, Milan Belica and Peter Chudík seized the opportunity to assume the position of Župan for the fourth consecutive term during the 2013 regional elections. Furthermore, the electoral success of Marian Kotleba, a prominent right-wing populist, in the Banská Bystrica region warrants separate discussion. The presence of such a figure in the highest administrative position in the region represents an electoral deviation in Slovak regional politics.

The 2017 regional elections marked a significant milestone since the inaugural elections in 2001. The election outcomes underscored a crisis within political parties and coalitions, as independent candidates secured first place in six out of eight regions (sharing first place with other political entities in the Košice region). This trend reflects a substantial level of distrust among Slovak voters towards traditional politicians. Furthermore, the decision to conduct the elections of Župans in a single round of voting, based on the principle of relative majority, represented a groundbreaking development. While this approach diminished the legitimacy of the newly elected Župans, it provided an opportunity for new candidates with minimal prospects in the second round of voting to emerge victorious. Consequently, the long-standing practice of "unlimited" tenure of office for Župans was discontinued, and six out of the eight Župans were elected for the first time.

The regional elections that took place in the Slovak Republic in 2022 revealed several important electoral trends. Firstly, there is a notable lack of trust in traditional political parties at the regional level. In contrast to the national level, the trend of depoliticization of regional authorities remains an important issue at the subregional level. The professional deputies of the Regional Assemblies must prioritize solving regional problems over political struggles. As a result, independent candidates played a significant role in the electoral preferences of Slovaks. However, when it comes to electing the Župan, party affiliation becomes the prevailing factor.

Secondly, the institution of independent deputies has garnered criticism for the degree of "independence" they possess, which is intended to distance the candidate from the influence of specific political parties. Some Slovakian political scientists have noted that independent deputies have voted alongside pro-government forces, despite having previously assured opposition during elections. Additionally, independent deputies have been reluctant to make unpopular decisions for the government in regional areas. At the regional level of governance in Slovakia, the factor of deputies' independence takes precedence over the party or ideological inclinations of the electorate.

Thirdly, the positions of Župans in self-governing regions can provide insight into the smallest dynamics of the political elite. In recent elections, six of the eight incumbent Župans were re-elected. One newly elected Župan, Ondrej Lunter, is the son of an influential politician in the region. Another newly elected Župan, Branislav Becík, won with a weakly legitimate 27% of the vote. Notably, independent candidates were not a significant factor in the election, with only Ondrej Lunter running as an independent. However, family ties were visible in this case.

Finally, the 2022 regional elections have shown a clear distinction between national and regional politics. Independent candidates are gaining popularity in regional elections, making the electoral process less partisan. However, there is a lack of rotation among regional political leaders.

In the 2022 elections, the cleavages between "Slovak Politics vs Hungarian Minority" and "Party vs Independent Deputies" played a significant role, similar to the previous elections. However, these cleavages have had different impacts on the election results and the political landscape of Slovak regions. The 2022 elections reaffirmed these differences and interim conclusions are expounded in the relevant chapters of the present monograph. It is apparent that holding regional and local elections simultaneously will only exacerbate the political fragmentation of the regions in the Slovak Republic. Amidst political turmoil, the advocacy for independent deputies is expected to surge, the Hungarian ethnic minority will likely seek support from Budapest, and the party Župans will manifest their allegiance to their respective parties to secure renomination. Concurrently, regional politics in the Slovak Republic evince a distinct political ecosystem, intricately intertwined with national politics.

References

1998 – Voľby do NR SR. Voľby a referendá. Available at: https://volby.statistics.sk/nrsr/nrsr1998/results/tab3.jsp.htm.

2001 – Voľby do orgánov samosprávnych krajov. Voľby a referendá. Available at: https://volby.statistics.sk/osk/osk2001/webdata/slov/home.htm.

2002 – Voľby do NR SR. Voľby a referendá. Available at: https://volby.statistics.sk/nrsr/nrsr2002/webdata/slov/graf/graf1.htm.

2003 – Účasť oprávnených občanov v referende. Voľby a referendá. Available at: https://volby.statistics.sk/ref/ref2003/webdata/sk/graf/graf1_ab.htm.

2005 – Voľby do orgánov samosprávnych krajov. Voľby a referendá. Available at: http://volby.statistics.sk/osk/osk2005/.

2009 – Voľby do orgánov samosprávnych krajov. Voľby a referendá. Available at: https://volby.statistics.sk/osk/osk2009/.

2012 – Voľby do NR SR. Voľby a referendá. Available at: https://volby.statistics.sk/nrsr/nrsr2012/sr/tab3.jsp@lang=sk.htm.

2013 – Voľby do orgánov samosprávnych krajov. Voľby a referendá. Available at: https://volby.statistics.sk/osk/osk2013/.

2013 – Évi XXXVI. Törvény a választási eljárásról. Hatályos Jogszabályok Gyűjteménye. Wolters Kluwer. Available at: https://net.jogtar.hu/jogszabaly?docid=a1300036.tv.

2016 – Voľby do NR SR. Voľby a referendá. Available at: https://volby.statistics.sk/nrsr/nrsr2016/sk/data02.html.

2017 – Voľby do orgánov samosprávnych krajov. Voľby a referendá. Available at: https://volby.statistics.sk/osk/osk2017/sk/.

Aktualizácia národnej stratégie regionálneho rozvoja Slovenskej republiky (pôvodná aktualizácia strategického dokumentu na roky 2014 až 2020). Podpora najmenej rozvinutých okresov a regionálny rozvoj. Bratislava, 2021. 177 p. Available at: https://www.vlada.gov.sk/data/files/6951_narodna_strategia_.pdf.

BAKKE, E., & SITTER, N. (2013). Why Do Parties Fail? Cleavages, Government Fatigue and Electoral Failure in the Czech Republic, Slovakia and Hungary 1992–2012. *East European Politics*. Vol. 29(2), pp. 208–225.

BAŠKA, Jaroslav – Minister obrany. Úrad vlády SR. 13.08.2024. Available at: https://www.nrsr.sk/web/Default.aspx?sid=poslanci/poslanec&PoslanecID=654&CisObdobia=6.

BAUER, Rudolf. MČ Košice – Západ. 12.04.2024. Available at: https://archiv.kosicezapad.sk/rndr-rudolf-bauer.

BECÍK, Branislav. O mne. 12.01.2024. Available at: https://branislavbecik.sk/o-mne/.

BELICA, Milan (SMER-SD, KDH, SDKÚ-DS, SNS), kandidát na župana v Nitrianskom kraji. SME.sk. 28.08.2009. Available at: https://domov.sme.sk/c/5038260/milan-belica-smer-sd-kdh-sdku-ds-sns-kandidat-na-zupana-v-nitrianskom-kraji.html.

BENKOVIČOVÁ, Ľ. (2006). Pohľad na vybrané otázky volieb do samosprávnych orgánov vyšších územných celkov v roku 2005. Slovenská politologická revue. No. 4. Available at: https://sjps.fsvucm.sk/Articles/06_4_2.pdf.

BLANÁR, Juraj. SMER – sociálna demokracia. 08.06.2024. Available at: https://stwebsmer.strana-smer.sk/juraj-blanar.

BRUSIS, M. (2008). Regionalisation in the Czech and Slovak Republics: Comparing the Influence of the European Union. In: *The Regional Challenge in Central and Eastern Europe, Territorial Restructuring and European Integration*. Michael Keating and James Hughes (eds). Paris: Peter Lang, pp. 89–105.

CIRNER, M., & DUDINSKÁ, I. (2018). Nepriame voľby ako alternatíva pre samosprávne kraje na Slovensku. In: *Politologická analýza regionálnych volieb 2017 na Slovensku*. Irina Dudinská, Michal Cirner, & Gabriel Székely (eds). Prešov: Vydavateľstvo Prešovskej university, pp. 50–57.

CSANYI, Peter (2024). Slovakia political briefing: The Election of the President of the Slovak Republic 2024. Weekly Briefing. China – CEE Institute. Vol. 72(1). Available at: https://china-cee.eu/wp-content/uploads/2024/05/2024p04_Slovakia.pdf.

DROBA, Juraj. Zoznam poslancov. Národná rada Slovenskej republiky. 18.08.2024. Available at: https://www.nrsr.sk/web/Default.aspx?sid=poslanci/poslanec&PoslanecID=780&CisObdobia=7.

Európske voľby 6. – 9. júna 2024. Európsky parlament. Available at: https://elections.europa.eu/sk/.

FAUVELLE-AYMAR, C., & STEGMAIER, M. (2008). Economic and Political Effects on European Parliamentary Electoral Turnout in Post-communist Europe. *Electoral Studies*. Vol. 27(4), pp. 661–672.

FREŠO, Pavol. Zoznam poslancov. Národná rada Slovenskej republiky. 09.07.2024. Available at: https://www.nrsr.sk/web/Default.aspx?sid=poslanci/poslanec&PoslanecID=654&CisObdobia=6.

Gašparovič založil politickú stranu Hnutie za demokraciu. SME Domov. 12.07.2002. Available at: https://domov.sme.sk/c/599832/gasparovic-zalozil-politicku-stranu-hnutie-za-demokraciu.html.

GYÁRFÁŠOVÁ, O., & HENDERSON, K. (2018). Slovakia and the Turnout Conundrum. *East European Politics*. Vol. 34(1), pp. 77–96.

HAAS, M. Report on the observation of the first regional elections held in Slovakia. 01.12.2001. Available at: https://aceproject.org/ero-en/regions/europe/SK/slovakia-report-on-the-observation-mision-first/at_download/file.

HAUGHTON, T. (2001). HZDS: The Ideology, Organisation and Support Base of Slovakia's Most Successful Party. *Europe-Asia Studies*. Vol. 53(5), pp. 745–769.

HAYDANKA, Y. (2021a). *Electoral Cleavages and Fragmentation of Regions in the Slovak Republic: A Case Study of the Parliamentary Elections Held in 1990–2020. Regionology*. Vol. 29(2), pp. 230–249.

HAYDANKA, Y. (2021b). *Notable Presidential Elections in the Slovak Republic: Institutional Design, Communication, and Cleavages*. Riga: Baltija Publishing.

História vlád SR. Úrad vlády SR. 12.04.2024. Available at: https://www.vlada. gov.sk/historia-vlad-sr/.

IBM Cognos Connection: Verejná databáza údajov. Statistical Office of the Slovak Republic. 31.01.2023. Available at: http://statdat.statistics.sk/cognosext.

Infographic: how many seats does each country get in the European Parliament? European Parliament 2024–2029. Available at: https://www.europarl. europa.eu/news/en/headlines/eu-affairs/20180126STO94114/infographic.

JAHELKA, T. (2021). Humanitná demokracia ako stále aktuálny koncept demokracie. In: *Kríza demokracie a nárast extrémistických nálad v Európe.* Lenka Diener & Tomáš Jahelka (eds). Trnava: Typi Universitatis Tyrnaviensis, pp. 160–175.

JANAS, K., & JÁNOŠKOVÁ, B. (2024). Comparison of Selected Aspects of Regional Self-Government in the V4 Countries. Medzinárodné Vzťahy. *Slovak Journal of International Relations.* Vol. 22(1), pp. 36–53.

JURINOVÁ, Erika. Zoznam poslancov. Národná rada Slovenskej republiky. 20.08.2024. Available at: https://www.nrsr.sk/web/Default.aspx?sid=poslanci/ poslanec&PoslanecID=795.

Jurinová a Viskupič sa vzdali poslaneckých mandátov. Trend.sk. 05.01.2018. Available at: https://www.trend.sk/spravy/jurinova-viskupic-vzdali-poslaneckych-mandatov.

KAPITÁN, Peter. Plavčan neodstúpil, zrušil výzvu na dlhodobý výskum. SME Domov. 14.08.2017. Available at: https://domov.sme.sk/c/20625878/plavcan-neodstupil-zrusil-vyzvu-na-dlhodoby-vyskum.html.

KDH. Predsedníctvo. 01.09.2024. Available at: https://kdh.sk/predsednictvo.

KNIŠ, Viktor. Dotujú Maďarov z mimoparlamentnej Aliancie orbánovci? Od začiatku sa vzájomne podporujú. REFRESHER – Svet modernej generácie. 07.0.2022. Available at: https://refresher.sk/115840-Dotuju-Madarov-z-mimoparlamentnej-Aliancie-orbanovci-Od-zaciatku-sa-vzajomne-podporuju.

KÖRBL, Hugo. Nové příležitosti pro slovenské občany z pohledu českého občanství a obráceně aneb česko-slovenské sblížení. Epravo.cz. 05.05.2022. Available at: https://www.epravo.cz/top/clanky/nove-prilezitosti-pro-slovenske-obcany-z-pohledu-ceskeho-obcanstvi-a-obracene-aneb-cesko-slovenske-sblizeni-114634.html.

Košice. Samospráva. 16.07.2024. Available at: https://www.kosice.sk/mesto/ samosprava.

KOTLEBA, Marian. Zoznam poslancov. Národná rada Slovenskej republiky. 15.08.2024. Available at: https://www.nrsr.sk/web/Page.aspx?sid=poslanci/po slanec&PoslanecID=944&CisObdobia=8.

KOVÁŘ, J. (2016). *Revisiting the Second-Order Election Model and Its Application to European Parliament Elections in Central and Eastern European Countries.* Prague: Metropolitan University Prague Press,.

KRIVÝ, V., FEGLOVÁ, V., & BALKO, D. Slovensko a jeho regióny: Sociokultúrne súvislosti volebného správania. Bratislava: Nadácia Médiá, 1996.

Kto komu pomôže? Nové pravidlá pre župné voľby prinášajú veľa otáznikov. Aktualne.sk. 06.11.2016. Available at: https://aktualne.atlas.sk/slovensko/politika/kto-pomoze-komu-nove-pravidla-zupne-volby-nechavaju-otazniky.html.

LUNTER, Ján. SME.sk. 02.05.2024. Available at: https://www.sme.sk/os/182929/ondrej-lunter.

LUNTER, Ondrej – Facebook. 30.08.2022. Available at: https://m.facebook.com/ondrejlunter/posts/462445959229748.

Maďari schválili dvojí občanství. Slováci pár hodin nato přišli s odvetou. iDNEScz. 26.04.2010. Available at: https://www.idnes.cz/zpravy/zahranicni/madari-schvalili-dvoji-obcanstvi-slovaci-par-hodin-nato-prisli-s-odvetou.A100526_094003_zahranicni_btw.

MAŇKA, Vladimír. MEPs European Parliament. 06.09.2024. Available at: https://www.europarl.europa.eu/meps/en/28192/VLADIMIR_MANKA/history/8.

MARTINKOVIČ, M. (2018). Regionálne voľby do VÚC ako prejav krízy funkčnosti strán v slovenskom straníckom systéme. In: *Politologická analýza regionálnych volieb 2017 na Slovensku*. Irina Dudinská, Michal Cirner, & Gabriel Székely (eds). Prešov: Vydavateľstvo Prešovskej university, pp. 39–49.

MARTINKOVIČ, M. (2021). *Coalition Governments and Development of the Party System in Slovakia*. Frankfurt am Main; Bratislava: Peter Lang, Veda.

MARUŠIAK, J. (2018). Regional Elections in Slovakia-a New Reformation of the Slovak Political Scene? *Contemporary European Studies*. No. 1, pp. 25–46.

MATOVIČ, Igor. Zoznam poslancov. Národná rada Slovenskej republiky. 19.08.2024. Available at: https://www.nrsr.sk/web/Default.aspx?sid=poslanci/poslanec&PoslanecID=773&CisObdobia=7.

My sme MOST-HÍD. 23.05.2024. Available at: https://www.mosthid.sk/.

NIŽŇANSKÝ, V., CIBÁKOVÁ, V., & HAMALOVÁ, M. (2014). *Tretia etapa decentralizácie verejnej správy na Slovensku*. Bratislava: Wolters Kluwer.

Nový rektor Technickej univerzity vo Zvolene. DrevMag. 05.11.2001. Available at: https://www.drevmag.com/index.php/cs/aktuality/1055-novy-rektor-technickej-univerzity-vo-zvolene.

NUTS Maps. Eurostat – 2023. Available at: https://ec.europa.eu/eurostat/web/nuts/nuts-maps.

OBCE SR – Základná mapa obcí Slovenskej republiky. 20.02.2024. Available at: http://www.sodbtn.sk/obce/obce_zaklad_mapa.php.

Osobný profil Jozef Viskupič. Aktuality.sk. 12.05.2023. Available at: https://www.aktuality.sk/osobnost/jozef-viskupic/.

Parlament schválil novelu zákona o štátnom občianstve. Ministerstvo vnútra Slovenskej republiky. 16.02.2022. Available at: https://www.minv.sk/?tlacove-spravy-8&sprava=parlament-schvalil-novelu-zakona-o-statnom-obcianstve.

SEYMOUR, Martin Lipset, & ROKKAN, Stein (eds) (1967). *Party Systems and Voter Alignments: Cross-National Perspectives*. New York: Free Press.

PATAJ, Roman. Kotleba buď prehrá, alebo bude za zbabelca. Dennik N.

16.07.2017. Available at: https://dennikn.sk/824951/kotleba-bud-prehra-alebo-bude-za-zbabelca/.

PETRUS, Peter. Na Slovensku pribudla nová politická strana Aliancia – Szövetség. Vznikla zlúčením viacerých subjektov. Noviny.sk. 02.10.2021. Available at: https://www.noviny.sk/slovensko/634464-na-slovensku-pribudla-nova-politicka-strana-aliancia-sz-vetseg-vznikla-zlucenim-viacerych-subjektov.

Počet obyvateľov podľa pohlavia vo všetkých krajoch SR k 1. 1. 2021. Scitanie.sk. Available at: https://www.scitanie.sk/obyvatelia/zakladne-vysledky/pocet-obyvatelov/SR/SK0/KR.

Politická strana ÚSVIT. 26.03.2024. Available at: https://usvit.estranky.sk/.

Poslanec Juraj Droba sa do SaS nevráti. Aktuality.sk. 12.8.2014. Available at: http://www.aktuality.sk/clanok/259441/droba-sa-do-sas-nevrati/.

REDŽIĆ, E., & EVERETT, J. (2020). Cleavages in the Post-Communist Countries of Europe: A Review. *Politics in Central Europe*. Vol. 16(1), pp. 231–258.

REHÁK, Oliver. SND podporí divadlá, ktorým Marian Kotleba stopol dotácie. Denník N. 06.10.2015. Available at: https://dennikn.sk/260887/snd-podpori-divadla-ktorym-marian-kotleba-stopol-dotacie/.

Slovak politics rocked by "Gorilla" corruption scandal. EURACTIV. 17.01.2012. Available at: https://www.euractiv.com/section/justice-home-affairs/news/slovak-politics-rocked-by-gorilla-corruption-scandal/.

Slovenskí politici reagujú na vojnu na Ukrajine: Útok odsúdili koalícia aj opozícia! Topky.sk. 22.02.2022. Available at: https://www.topky.sk/cl/10/2267829/Slovenski-politici-reaguju-na-VOJNU-na-Ukrajine–Utok-odsudili-koalicia-aj-opozicia.

Sme reports that Labour Minister Richter's diploma was not signed by the dean. The Slovak Spectator. 07.05.2012. Available at: https://spectator.sme.sk/c/20043357/sme-reports-that-labour-minister-richters-diploma-was-not-signed-by-the-dean.html.

SMER-SD. Slovenská sociálna demokracia. 07.05.2024. Available at: https://www.strana-smer.sk/o-nas/o-nas.

SÓLYMOS, K. K., FINTA, M., CUPRIK, R., & DIKO, L. Maďarské peniaze pre slovenský juh: Milióny v mene budúcich hlasov? Investigatívne Centrum Jána Kuciaka. 26.02.2021. Available at: https://www.icjk.sk/103/Madarske-peniaze-pre-slovensky-juh-Miliony-v-mene-buducich-hlasov.

Starosta Petržalky Bajan už kandidovať nebude. SME Bratislava. 11.09.2018. Available at: https://bratislava.sme.sk/c/20911477/starosta-petrzalky-bajan-znova-kandidovat-nebude.html.

Strana Aliancia. 16.01.2023. Available at: https://strana-aliancia.sk/.

Strana rómskej koalície. Facebook. 08.07.2024. Available at: https://www.facebook.com/p/Strana-r%C3%B3mskej-koal%C3%ADcie-100068212406920/.

Survey: Record turnout at European elections driven by young people. Emerging Europe. 26.09 2019. Available at: https://emerging-europe.com/news/record-turnout-at-european-elections-driven-by-young-people/.

SZABÓ, B., & TÁTRAI, P. (2016). Regional and Social Cleavages in the Slovak Elections After the Change of the Regime. *Geografický časopis*. Vol. 68(3), pp. 195–212.

TARČÁK, Jozef. Zoznam poslancov. Národná rada Slovenskej republiky. 08.06.2024. Available at: https://www.nrsr.sk/web/Default.aspx?sid=poslanci/poslanec&PoslanecID=136&CisObdobia=4.

Tibor Mikuš dnes nastupuje do funkcie predsedu TTSK. SME Domov. 09.01.2016. Available at: https://domov.sme.sk/c/2537916/tibor-mikus-dnes-nastupuje-do-funkcie-predsedu-ttsk.html.

TRNKA, Rastislav. Tím Trnka. 19.02.2024. Available at: https://www.rastotrnka.sk/.

Trvalý pobyt na päť rokov. Migračné informačné centrum IOM. 22.07.2024. Available at: https://www.mic.iom.sk/sk/pobyt2/trvaly-pobyt/169-trvaly-pobyt-na-pat-rokov.html.

Turnout by Year – European Parliament (2004–2024). European Union. Available at: https://results.elections.europa.eu/en/turnout/.

Ústavný zákon č. 460/1992 Ústava Slovenskej republiky. Zákony pre ľudí – SK. Available at: https://www.zakonypreludi.sk/zz/1992-460.

VOITOVYCH, V. (2023). Local and Regional Elections in Slovakia in 2022: The Impact on the Inter-party Balance and Structuring of the Political Space. National Technical University of Ukraine. *Journal of Political Science, Sociology & Law*. Vol. 1(57), pp. 62–70.

Voľby a referendá. Štatistický úrad SR. Available at: https://volby.statistics.sk/.

Voľby do orgánov samosprávy obcí a voľby do orgánov samosprávnych krajov konané v rovnaký deň a v rovnakom čase v roku 2022. Ministerstvo vnútra Slovenskej republiky. Available at: https://www.minv.sk/?volby-selfgov22.

Volebné preferencie politických strán. Fokus. 2022–2023. Available at: https://www.focus-research.sk/.

VRAŽDA, Daniel. Kotleba je podľa starostov najhorší žiak v župe. 28.09.2015. Denník N. Available at: https://dennikn.sk/253171/kotleba-najhorsi-ziak-zupe/.

WHITEFIELD, S. (2002). Political Cleavages and Post-communist Politics. *Annual Review of Political Science*. Vol. 5, pp. 181–200.

Zákon č. 80/1990 Sb. Zákon Slovenskej národnej rady o voľbách do Slovenskej národnej rady. Zákony pro lidi – Sbírka zákonů ČR. Available at: https://www.zakonyprolidi.cz/cs/1990-80.

Zákon č. 369/1990. Zákon Slovenskej národnej rady o obecnom zriadení. Zákony pre ľudí – SK. Available at: https://www.zakonypreludi.sk/zz/1990-369.

Zákon č. 221/1996 Národnej Rady Slovenskej Republiky z 3. júla 1996 o územnom a správnom usporiadaní Slovenskej republiky. SLOV-LEX. Available at: https://www.slov-lex.sk/pravne-predpisy/SK/ZZ/1996/221/.

Zákon č. 302/2001 zo 4. júla 2001 o samospráve vyšších územných celkov (zákon o samosprávnych krajoch). SLOV-LEX. Available at: https://www.slov-lex.sk/pravne-predpisy/SK/ZZ/2001/302/.

Zákon č. 303/2001 zo 4. júla 2001 o voľbách do orgánov samosprávnych krajov a o doplnení Občianskeho súdneho poriadku. SLOV-LEX. Available at: https://www.slov-lex.sk/pravne-predpisy/SK/ZZ/2001/303/vyhlasene_znenie.html.

Zákon č. 180/2014. Zákon o podmienkach výkonu volebného práva a o zmene a doplnení niektorých zákonov. Zákony pre ľudí – SK. Available at: https://www.zakonypreludi.sk/zz/2014-180.

Zákon č. 185/2022. Zákon o špeciálnom spôsobe hlasovania vo voľbách do orgánov samosprávy obcí a vo voľbách do orgánov samosprávnych krajov, ktoré sa konajú v roku 2022 v rovnaký deň a v rovnakom čase a ktorým sa menia a dopĺňajú niektoré zákony. Zákony pre ľudí – SK. Available at: https://www.zakonypreludi.sk/zz/2022-185.

Zaslúžite si mať sa lepšie. KDH Program. 19.02.2024. Available at: https://kdh.sk/.

Životopis predsedu VÚC Trenčianskeho samosprávneho kraja Š. Štefanca. SME Domov. 16.12.2001. Available at: https://domov.sme.sk/c/187419/zivotopis-predsedu-vuc-trencianskeho-samospravneho-kraja-s-stefanca.html.

Zomrel bývalý predseda Trenčianskeho kraja Sedláček. 27.04.2015. MY MY Trenčín. Available at: https://mytrencin.sme.sk/c/7774340/zomrel-byvaly-predseda-trencianskeho-kraja-sedlacek.html.

Zomrel herec, politik a bývalý minister kultúry Ľubo Roman. Ministerstvo kultúry Slovenskej republiky. 14.03.2022. Available at: https://www.culture.gov.sk/ministerstvo/medialny-servis/aktuality-ministerstva-kultury/zomrel-herec-politik-a-byvaly-minister-kultury-lubo-roman/.

Župné voľby budú začiatkom novembra. Predseda Národnej rady Andrej Danko stanovil dátum župných volieb. SME. 23.06.2017. Available at: https://domov.sme.sk/c/20566195/volby-do-vyssich-uzemnych-celkov-budu-zaciatkom-novembra.html.